W9-AFD-111

Additional praise for *To the Last Salute*:

"[Elizabeth Campbell] has provided readers of naval history and popular culture something of great utility, and great fun: an English translation of her famous ancestor's World War I memoir. . . . Trapp's book gives us a rare glimpse into the world of the earlier submariner, and of a naval force that no longer exists. . . . An entertaining story that gives the reader a vivid picture of submarine warfare at its most primitive."—Donald Stoker, *Journal of Military History*

"[Georg von Trapp] almost certainly always tried to put his best foot forward, and he emerges from his account as a man of great skill, considerable compassion . . . and sufficient tact and tolerance to handle the kind of polyglot crews that sailed for the Dual Monarchy. . . . He fought on to the end, knowing that the Dual Monarchy he served so well was crumbling. In the end, he gave the last salute of the title when the imperial flag was hauled down for the last time. Appealing to von Trapp family admirers, of course, and also to naval buffs, regardless of how they respond to music."—*Booklist*

"This book is the hitherto untold prequel to the legendary von Trapp history. In his narrative Captain von Trapp emerges as a patriot, a compassionate commander, and a self-effacing hero."—William Anderson, author of *The World of the Trapp Family*

Captain Georg Ritter von Trapp, 1935

GEORG VON TRAPP

To the Last
Salute

Memories of an Austrian U-Boat Commander

Translated and with an introduction by

ELIZABETH M. CAMPBELL

With an essay by

ROBERT C. LENDT

University of Nebraska Press
Lincoln & London

Translation and introduction © 2007 by Elizabeth M. Campbell Peters
"The World of *To the Last Salute*" © 2007 by the Board of Regents
of the University of Nebraska

All photographs are reprinted from Georg von Trapp's *Bis zum letzten
Flaggenschuss* (Salzburg, 1935).

Library of Congress Cataloging-in-Publication Data
Trapp, Georg von, 1880–1947.
[Bis zum letzten Flaggenschuss. English]
To the last salute: memories of an Austrian U-Boat commander /
Georg von Trapp; translated and with an introduction by
Elizabeth M. Campbell; with an essay by Robert C. Lendt.
p. cm.
Includes bibliographical references.
ISBN-13: 978-0-8032-4667-6 (cl.: alk. paper)
ISBN-10: 0-8032-4667-6 (cl.: alk. paper)
ISBN-13: 978-0-8032-1350-0 (pa.: alk. paper)
1. Trapp, Georg von, 1880–1947. 2. Austro-Hungarian Monarchy.
Kriegsmarine. K.u.K. Unterseeboot-Waffe—Biography.
3. World War, 1914–1918—Naval operations—Submarine.
4. World War, 1914–1918—Naval operations, Austrian.
5. World War, 1914–1918—Personal narratives, Austrian.
6. Submarine captains—Austria—Biography. I. Title.
D595.A8T713 2007
940.4′512092—dc22
[B]
2006024418

Contents

List of Illustrations

LIST OF ILLUSTRATIONS

Preface

I never knew my grandfather Georg von Trapp; he died in 1947 when my mother, Eleonore "Lorli," was sixteen. She speaks of him with great affection; her voice often wavers and tears fill her eyes as she tells stories about him and her pride in his accomplishments. He was supportive of her when no one else was, and was always loving and affectionate. This made his loss all the more poignant. In my mother's mind and heart, Papá stood way above everyone else in the family. So I decided to read his book in order to learn more about him. The more I read, the more I wanted others to know his story. The book was originally published in Austria in 1935, in German, and has been out of print for sixty-seven years. This is the first English translation, though originally it was translated into French.

What makes my grandfather's book so appealing is the simplicity with which he writes. His modesty underscores the events that occur and the famous people he meets. He was the most successful submarine captain in the Austro-Hungarian navy, but he was always self-effacing. He never let his work interfere with his family. By the end of World War I, there were five von Trapp children; two more were born after the Armistice.

When his career as a navy captain ended with the defeat of Austria in the war and Austria's loss of coastline, he was crushed. His love for his country was so strong that it melded into his own identity. Part of him died when he lowered the Austro-Hungarian flag for the last time.

While researching this book, I spent time talking with my mother, Lorli (Eleonore) Trapp Campbell, and her living siblings, Werner, Agathe, Maria, Rosmarie, and Johannes von Trapp. Like my mother, his children were all close to him and loved him a great deal. Their research, stories, and impressions helped me to understand my grandfather better. My deepest thanks to all of them. Agathe has written a book called *Memories Before and After the* Sound of Music (PublishAmerica, 2004), which I recommend for more details of their family life.

There are two reasons why I wanted to translate this book: one, to let my children become acquainted with the extraordinary man who was their great-grandfather; and two, to rectify the false image of him portrayed onscreen and onstage. It is my hope that reading his memoir will bring to life the real Georg von Trapp for you too.

Acknowledgments

I owe a sincere debt of gratitude to the following people without whom this translation of my grandfather's book would never have been published.

To my parents, Hugh and Eleonore "Lorli" Campbell, for their unwavering encouragement and assistance.

To my aunts Agathe and Maria von Trapp, and to Mary Louise Kane, for their sharp eyes and ears, their impressive perseverance, and their good humor; may I be blessed with those qualities when I am in my nineties.

To Karl Dillmann, for naval terms and historical accuracy.

To Bill Anderson, for endless, positive suggestions.

To Polly Chatfield, the best godmother ever.

To my sisters Jeanie Lero and Peggy Freeman, and to dear friends Barbara Post, Pia Centenari-Leonard, Betsey Mayhew, Jackie Willey, Cynthia Meisner, and Susan Polk, I treasure you all.

Finally, to my children, Nathaniel and Molly, during whose lives this book has been an ongoing project, for not minding burned and late dinners and my using the computer when they needed it, too. You make my heart soar and life worth living. I will always love you deeply.

> For thus says the Lord God, the Holy One of Israel:
> In returning and rest you shall be saved;
> In quietness and in trust shall be your strength.
>
> ISAIAH 30:15

Introduction

Meet the Real Captain von Trapp

Georg Johannes Ritter von Trapp was born in Zara on the Dalmatian coast, then Austrian territory, on April 4, 1880, to August and Hedwig Wepler von Trapp. He had a sister Hedwig and a brother Werner. August von Trapp was an Austrian naval officer, who died of typhoid fever when Georg was only four years old. His widow, Hedwig, managed to raise her three children on a small pension, moving first to her mother's home in Eisenach, Germany, and then to Graz, Austria, where the children went to school.

Georg went to the naval academy in Fiume to learn to be an officer. In those days the schooling included etiquette, dancing, and violin lessons because the officers were allowed to go to social events, including court balls. They needed to know correct behavior and appropriate conversation for such occasions.

As was the custom, Georg's graduating class sailed around the world in a schooner. They got as far as Australia and then went up the coast of China, taking measurements (for their maps, no doubt). They did not continue across the Pacific but went home the way they had come. They stopped in Egypt, where a fortuneteller grabbed Georg's hand and predicted, "You will have two wives, you will have ten children, you will see two world wars, and you will live to be one hundred years old." He was shocked at these improbable predictions, especially since he had not sought her advice in the first place. Ironically, all but the last one came true, though when given, each seemed more unlikely than the next.

In the Holy Land, Georg met a Franciscan monk who took him on a tour of all the Biblical sights he wanted to see. Among other things, Georg bought seven bottles of Jordan water; they were later used to baptize his first seven children.

In 1908 Georg was commissioned by the Austrian navy to study the design and construction of torpedoes and submarines at the Whitehead factory in Fiume.[1] While in Fiume, he was invited to a party where Agathe Breunner Whitehead played the piano and her daughter Agathe played the violin.[2] It was love at first sight. Agathe invited Georg to visit her family's summer home at Zell am See, Austria. Their summer home was a chalet named the Erlhof, with a spectacular view of the alp called the Kitzsteinhorn. Georg and Agathe continued to see each other, attending balls and parties during the social seasons of Pola, Trieste, and Fiume.

When *U-5* was to be launched for the first time in 1909, Agathe was chosen to christen the vessel; standing close by on the platform was Kapitänleutnant von Trapp.[3] Coincidentally, Georg commanded the *U-5* a few years later in the war.

The romance between Agathe and Georg continued at the leisurely pace that was customary in those days. They were married on January 10, 1911, and lived in the Trapp villa in Pola, Austria.

Their first child, Rupert Georg von Trapp, was born November 1, 1911, in Pola; Agathe followed on March 12, 1913. When Maria Francisca arrived on September 28, 1914, Agathe sent her husband a telegram to inform him, but because of the war, personal telegrams to the military were not allowed. They had agreed ahead of time on a code, so she telegrammed, "S.M.S. *Maria* arrived."[4]

Papá, as his children referred to him, was much beloved as a father. His children remember him romping around with them, playing Indians with them, and teaching them simple songs the navy men sang.[5] When he came home on leave from the war, they remember being quiet so he could sleep, and then, when they couldn't wait any longer, singing outside his door to awaken him. But when the leave was over, there was never any dramatic good-bye. He was suddenly gone, and then, just as suddenly, he appeared during his next leave.

During the war Georg's family moved to Zell am See, to the Whitehead family's Erlhof. It was a safe haven, with a self-sustaining farm, outbuildings for laundry, wood, an ice cellar, a gardener's house, a farmhouse, and stables. It had a dock and a boathouse on the lake since trips to town (directly across the lake) were made by boat.

As an English citizen, grandmother Agathe Whitehead was allowed to remain on her property during the war but not to leave the country. Food was scarce, even though the Whiteheads grew a big garden. Bread was made of corn, not wheat, so the groceries Georg was able to bring home on furlough (described in "Sheet Lightning") were most welcome.

Three more children were born at Zell am See during the war, Werner on December 21, 1915; Hedwig on July 17, 1917; and Johanna on September 7, 1919. At the Erlhof there was neither radio nor electricity, and the telephone was primitive, used by adults only for important messages.

After the war Georg came back to Zell am See. Agathe told the children, "You must be very sweet and kind to Papá because he lost the war and the Navy." Too young to understand fully what had happened, they obeyed because they loved their father so much.

At this point the von Trapp household was comprised of two parents, five children, a nanny for the younger ones, and a governess for the older ones. With grandmother Whitehead's own staff, the Erlhof was just not large enough for such a large group.

In 1921 Georg and Agathe moved their family to Kloster-neuburg, outside Vienna. Shortly after they moved in, Martina was born, on February 17, 1921. Not long after that Agathe, the oldest daughter, came down with scarlet fever. Her siblings also contracted the disease, and their mother nursed them. Then she became ill herself. She was sick for nine months and eventually went to a sanitarium in Vienna. When she returned she was in a wheelchair, and a week later she died, on September 3, 1922.

The whole family was stunned by her death. With the loss of his career and the death of his wife, Georg felt completely devastated. Although many other challenges occurred in his life, he never recovered fully from these two shocks. Somehow he mustered strength to create a loving, secure environment for his seven children.

Restless, Georg asked the two eldest, Rupert and Agathe, if they would like to move to a Pacific island. There would be bananas and coconuts there, he encouraged. But the children had been taught religious education by their governess, and she had impressed upon them the need for weekly Mass. Rupert asked his father if there would be a church there. When his father said, "No," the children said that they could not move there. A few minutes later Papá suggested, "How about Salzburg? My friend Seyffertitz lives there."[6]

Outside Salzburg, in the suburb of Aigen, Georg remodeled a villa that was large enough for his family. In 1924 they moved in. He built a log house in the garden for the children to play in, he planted a big garden, and he raised chickens. He even bought a huge dog and harnessed a cart to it so little Martina could go for rides. As depicted in *The Sound of Music*, Georg did have a bosun's whistle, but he did not use it in the militaristic manner portrayed in the film. During the war he had needed that whistle on the submarine to send orders when noise and smoke interfered. He couldn't shout loud enough, so he whistled commands. In Aigen he gave each child a signal because the grounds were so extensive. There was also a whistle signal for everyone to come at once.

In the summers he took the older children camping with their cousins and uncle. The adults brought along their musical instruments so there would be a quartet of two violins, guitar, and accordion playing music late into the evening at the campsite. As a result the children wanted to learn how to play the instruments. When they came home, Agathe learned guitar, Rupert and Maria the accordion, and Werner the viola da gamba. They also sang the simple songs the sailors had created during the war. Music-making and singing were important activities in their early childhood.

Maria remembers that Georg was "a very fatherly father. He did everything for us. He was the happiest when we were very young. We could turn his study upside down, turn the chairs over and put a blanket over them to make a house and totally mess up his room. He took us on trips and we'd make a fire and bake potatoes in the coals, and when we were sick he would always be at our bedside. When I had diphtheria and was partially paralyzed, he would sit beside my bed. Every night he would come into [our] room and tell us a story that went on and on and on. He must have had a terrific imagination, but we took it for granted.

"When I wanted to play the accordion, he gave me an accordion. When I wanted to play the violin, he let me have Mamá's violin. I didn't want lessons; I wanted to learn from him. He couldn't teach me enough. As soon as I could play even a little, we had a little family quintet. We played every night. He was a really good father."

In Aigen the children walked to school; eventually they were given bicycles to save time. But these trips to school proved too much for Maria, still weak from scarlet fever and diphtheria. Georg contacted the nuns at Nonnberg Abbey, who told him about Maria Augusta Kutschera, who could tutor Maria. This is where the story told in my grandmother's book, *The Story of the Trapp Family Singers* and later in *The Sound of Music* has its start.

"Gustl," as the tutor was called, belonged to a group of students who made music together as they traveled through Austria. They sang madrigals and sacred songs that she taught the von Trapp children. At this time Papá was "semiengaged" to a woman he knew through some relatives, but she was continually postponing a wedding, saying that her wardrobe wasn't ready or other excuses. Papá had always told his children that if he remarried it would be to someone with an interest in his children. Georg saw his children bond to Gustl, and since she was an orphan, she enjoyed being a part of the family. Georg and Gustl became engaged.

Georg got an offer from an American businessman to take a ship from Bremen to Genoa, so he took the job. Gustl stayed with the children while he was gone, taking them for hikes, teaching them volleyball, and, of course, singing. When Papá returned from that trip, he and Gustl were married, on November 26, 1927. After their wedding, the family continued their hobby of group singing with Gustl. In 1929 Rosmarie was born; two years later Eleonore (Lorli) arrived. A bank failure soon after wiped out the family fortune. The once wealthy von Trapps had to live very economically.

The Salzburg Music Festival was an annual August event, so to raise money, the family rented their house to festival-goers and vacationed on the Adriatic island called Veruda on the Dalmatian coast. It was a paradise for them! They slept in hammocks hung between trees, burned dried dung for firewood, bought fish and milk from the local people, and lived simply. They took a boat to go to church every Sunday and were treated to gelato afterward on the hot days. During the second summer trip they bought Klepper folding boats that held two people and had orange and red sails. Now they were able to take overnight trips from Veruda into the Adriatic Sea. The older children went once on a three-day and then a ten-day trip down the Yugoslavian coast. The third year Papá rented a sailing vessel, the *Archimedes*, and they went down the coast toward Albania, back to Veruda, then to Venice. All the children have fond memories of these vacations and emphasize how much their father enjoyed both the simple lifestyle and showing them the Adriatic and the coast that he knew so well.

Rosmarie remembers her father calming her terrible nightmares as a child. "He always had a simple answer because he was used to being a commander and finding the quickest, the surest answer to all the problems. And he had this genius for solving problems. He had a big, compassionate heart."

Lorli remembers the stories he told her and Rosmarie when they were children. He would push back his chair and take one child on each knee and tell of a "friendly giant who would reach into our third-story bedroom window and put us in his ear. We would hang onto his hair there and he would take us on trips. In two steps he would be through the Mediterranean and we would end up in the Sahara. We always ended up in the Sahara! And the giant would walk around and take a nap, always at an oasis. We would go and eat dates and there would always be a lion that would come and attack us, and the giant would wake up just in time. And then he would take us back and deposit us back at the dormer of our room on the third floor."

Georg must have written the original *Bis zum letzten Flagen-schuss*, or *To the Last Salute*, during this time because it was published in 1935 by the publishing house Anton Pustet of Salzburg. Both Agathe and daughter Maria remember him typing it. My grandmother helped him organize the sequence of the chapters and write the first chapter, but he wrote the manuscript himself.

Also during this time the family began singing at the church in Aigen, where they met Dr. Franz Wasner, a priest who recognized their musical talent. What began as informal critiquing from him became rehearsals as he taught them sacred music as well as folk songs, madrigals, and ballads. The singer Lotte Lehman heard them at the Villa Trapp in 1935 and insisted they sing at the Salzburg Festival in the song competition. They won a prize. After that The Trapp Family Choir, as they became known, received invitations to sing at other venues, including Belvedere Palace in Vienna and the Mozarteum in Salzburg, and to perform a concert tour in France, Belgium, Holland, Italy, Germany, and England.[7]

Simultaneously, Hitler began muscling Austria and other European nations into submission to Germany. In Aigen, Georg received two letters inviting him to join Hitler's navy. Georg knew that a third letter would never arrive but that Hitler's men would simply arrive to take him to a new post. He was adamant about not working for Hitler, and he and my grandmother knew they had no choice but to leave.

Eleonore's memory reinforces her father's feelings at this time. "Once—it must have been at the Anschluss—my father's frustration came out.[8] The giant waded into the Atlantic Ocean and he would pick up these German warships and he would hold them between his fingers and with his thumb he would break them in half. And the German sailors would be swimming in the water, he said, 'like flies.' They would hang onto the hair on the giant's legs, and the hair on a giant's leg is like the line on a ship. The giant would raise his leg and scrape them off with a swipe of his hand, and then he would take us home. At the time I was just bug-eyed, but in retrospect it was the time of the Anschluss and he was just trying to get even with those Nazis who were driving us out of our country."

As his children now look back on the family's strengths and weaknesses in the years in Europe, they see how both parents had a role in bringing the family out of Austria. Daughter Maria remembers the whole family talking about the possibility of going to America. They "would go only if everyone agreed; if one person disagreed, we would not go. Papá asked each one of us and each one said, 'Yes.' Then he took a big Bible to see what the Word of God said. He'd never done this before. He wanted to make sure that it was God's will that we go to America. He closed his eyes, took a pencil, and opened to the place where God tells Abraham, 'Take your family and go to the land I have chosen for you.'

"It was clear that Hitler was wrong. Papá knew that he could not serve Hitler; he had convictions about what is right and what is wrong," remembers Maria. Eleonore says, "God gave Papá the convictions and the integrity and the discernment. He gave Mother the gumption and the courage to carry it out because it really took a driving force to get us out of that country." Agathe adds, "She was the force who put into action what God told us to do."

In 1938 the family secretly left Austria with their musical conductor, Dr. Franz Wasner. They arrived in New York nearly penniless. Almost immediately they started touring as a concert group. Gradually The Trapp Family Singers became well known. They toured the United States to increasing acclaim. Their hobby became their profession.

Georg accompanied the family on all their travels from concert hall to concert hall. He was supportive in the backstage details, though he did not sing onstage. It was a completely new role for him, but his calming presence was vital as the family fulfilled their rigorous performing schedule.

In 1941 the family had enough money to buy a new home in America, a farm in Stowe, Vermont. Now, as the children recall building their home there, they remember their father as a quiet man who always encouraged them through the difficult times. "He was not a disciplinarian," remembers Werner. "He tried to lead us on vacations that were a more natural way of living, not in hotels. When we started singing, he could have said no, but he withdrew so we could blossom. It was a strong way of showing us but not really forcing his ideas on us."

"I met some of his sailors once in Austria, and they had nothing but praise for him. And Mamá, too. Everyone says how gentle she was, always helpful and thinking of others. I remember her only as very kind," Maria says.

"He nurtured, he supported the family, he encouraged," Eleonore remembers. "He brought out the best in you. You wanted to please him, and that's why Croats, Yugoslavs, all these nationalities got along together on his submarines. There was no problem; they loved him; they got along beautifully."

Eleonore remembers that "in Vermont he got more and more quiet. He worked as much as we all did; we all worked on the house, but often he would sit on the porch and just look out at the Green Mountains. There was always a reflective but a sad look on his face—more and more withdrawn. But I just loved him to pieces."

"We didn't even know he was a war hero. We knew what he did, but we never thought it was anything extraordinary. He never impressed this upon us. We were just children of the Captain," Agathe recalls. This was typical of his modesty.

Georg died of lung cancer at home in Stowe on May 30, 1947; he is buried in the family cemetery there. Ironically his cancer was caused, in part, by the fumes he inhaled while on his submarines. At the time of his death, his family was singing to him. Although his death wrenched their hearts, what he said and did as a father enriched them all their lives; they still refer to the lessons he taught them. I hope that his legacy of bravery, kindness, and perseverance is a bright thread through his memoir of life as a submarine captain.

The World of *To the Last Salute*

ROBERT C. LENDT

The world that Georg von Trapp was born into was transformed by the war in which he distinguished himself in the service of the Austro-Hungarian Empire. The First World War marked the end of the era of powerful European monarchies with the collapse of the Hapsburg, Hohenzollern, and Romanov dynasties and created conditions of social and political unrest that set the stage for further twentieth-century conflict in Europe and elsewhere.

The European continent had been without major wars since the Napoleonic conflicts ended in 1815. The hundred years of relative peace, however, had not been without tension as the great European powers developed throughout the nineteenth century. Most countries were affected by great waves of liberal or nationalistic unrest that swept through Europe in the first half of the century, and the Austrian Empire, home of Georg von Trapp, was reorganized and its policy greatly influenced as a result of these forces.

The Austrian Empire was made up of dozens of nationalities, which currently inhabit numerous independent nations in central and eastern Europe. These nationalities were held together in the person of the Emperor of Austria who ruled over what one commentator called "a melting pot on a cold stove." The people of these nationalities, especially the Hungarians and the Slavic peoples of the Balkan region, increasingly agitated for autonomy or independence from the ethnic Germans of Austria as the century progressed. This desire for nationhood increased after Austria's defeat in a war with Prussia in 1866. The Austrian defeat not only set the stage for the creation of the German Empire but also resulted in the modification of the

.trian government. Weakened by their loss, the Austrians .anted considerable autonomy to the Hungarian portions of their empire as exemplified by their nation's new name. From 1867, the Dual Monarchy of Austria-Hungary was created with the Emperor Franz Josef ruling as both the Emperor of Austria and the King of Hungary (Thus the K.u.K. abbreviation in the text—Kaiserliche und Könige [Emperor and King]). This concession of course encouraged other minority groups in the empire to increase their demands for freedom as well. As will be seen in Captain von Trapp's account, relations between these nationalities within the empire became cause for growing concern as the war continued and reached critical proportions by the end of the conflict.

Thwarted in central Europe by the growing power of Germany, the Austrians attempted to extend their influence into southeastern Europe, where they annexed the region of Bosnia-Herzegovina by 1907. This action not only increased the number of discontented nationalities within Austria-Hungary but also ensured conflict with Russia, whose ambitions included domination of the Balkan region, including the Turkish straits and Serbia, which saw itself as the nucleus of a Yugoslav state.

In addition to nationalism, several other factors created conditions that led to World War I. Imperialist competition in overseas regions caused tension to rise, especially among Germany, Britain, and France, which argued over territories on the African continent and elsewhere. As has been seen, Austria-Hungary and Russia were in conflict in the Balkans, and the Russians were also eager to expand at the expense of the Ottoman Empire, the so-called Sick Man of Europe. These expansionist tendencies fueled a growing militarism that resulted in a naval arms race in which Germany and Britain played leading roles, and all nations expanded their land forces through training of reserves, creation of general staffs, and the development of military plans to allow for instantaneous reaction to any crisis. In the quest for security in this dangerous environment, all of the major powers sought protection in alliances that were, in reality, mutual defense treaties. By 1914 two major alliances were in place. The Triple Alliance united Germany, Austria-Hungary, and Italy (in spite of their earlier war, Germany and Austria were still influenced by their common German heritage), and after a series of alliances, the Triple Entente made up of Great Britain, France, and Russia came into being. The peace of Europe came increasingly to rest on the complex relationships between these great powers.

In August 1914, the century of general peace came to an end with the assassination of the Austrian Archduke Franz Ferdinand and his wife in Sarajevo, Bosnia. Their murder at the hands of a Bosnian member of a Serbian nationalistic secret society set in motion the sequence of events that saw most of the major European powers at war within a month. Austria-Hungary, by declaring war on Serbia, forced Russia's hand, and the Tsar ordered a general mobilization of his huge army in order to defend their fellow Slavs in Serbia. The Germans, feeling threatened by Russian mobilization of their reserves, declared war on Russia, and in keeping with a long-standing plan to prosecute a two-front war by attacking France first, declared war on their Russian ally as well. When, according to the same plan, the German army invaded the neutral nation of Belgium, the British reacted by declaring war on Germany. The Italians, citing the defensive nature of the Triple Alliance, remained neutral initially.

As the war developed, Germany and Austria-Hungary (later joined by the Ottoman Empire and Bulgaria) came to be called the Central Powers. Britain, France, and Russia were known as the Allied Powers and were eventually joined by dozens of nations from around the world including the United States. Persuaded by Allied promises of Austro-Hungarian coastal cities along the Adriatic Sea, Italy switched sides and joined the Allies in May of 1915, thereby becoming an operational zone for Captain von Trapp's Austrian submarine.

The submarines, or U-boats, that Captain von Trapp commanded had been under development only since the 1890s and had never been used in large numbers in the history of warfare. These vessels were very unlike modern submarines that can remain submerged indefinitely and whose speed while submerged is equal to or greater than their speed on the surface. Austro-Hungarian submarines in 1914 were small, crowded, unreliable, and designed to operate on the surface most of the time. Underwater operations were initially used mainly for the purpose of evasion. On the surface the Central Power's U-boats were powered by diesel engines (the older Austrian models used gasoline engines, however) and could travel at 12 to 14 knots in good conditions, although some smaller types were slower. The ships could be ventilated during surface cruising, ensuring that the negative effects of engine exhaust on the crew would be minimized. The batteries for use in operating the electric motors that powered the ships when they submerged (no atmospheric air being available for use in the internal combustion engines) could also be recharged at this time. Submerged, these U-boats could at best make only two-thirds of their speed on the surface and could remain underwater only as long as air quality permitted or electric power in the batteries remained. Of course, the faster the submarine traveled underwater, the more quickly the batteries became discharged. As a result of these limitations, surface attacks with deck guns (which also conserved valuable torpedoes) were preferred in the early war period. As antisubmarine defenses improved, however, U-boats had to resort to submerging more frequently for self-preservation.

Since submarine warfare was in its infancy in World War I, in the war's early days certain conventions were put in place to conform with international law. These included the need to identify a ship's nationality prior to attack, the firing of warning shots to cause the target to stop, inspections for contraband on board, and giving the opportunity for the crew to abandon ship before its destruction. All of these restrictions were abandoned with time as the grim reality of the submarine war's destructive nature became clear for all to see. It was this policy of unrestricted submarine warfare that became a pivotal factor in the decision of the United States to enter the war.

All of these issues made service in early submarines challenging and hazardous, but as the account of his war experience reveals, courageous leaders such as Captain von Trapp rose to the challenge and served their nations with bravery and honor.

they form
that look
lackberry

the cot-
w deep
water

with-
the
and
is a
ike
c
who waded down the length of the coast and carried a

s docked in Sebenico amid her ni
division.[1]

night searching for enemy ships that had
ice again, had found nothing.

Adriatic we had investigated, looked, and
came back disappointed through the "Incoro-
en, rocky islands that extend in front of the harbor

uld have been called the "Thousand Islands" as they
ered about there. The people tell how there was once
who waded down the length of the coast and carried a
ack full of stones. At one point he noticed that his sack had
st and that he had lost half of them. He threw the rest angrily
ward Sebenico and took off. There were big and little stones;
some of them became actual, respectable islands with mountains. Signal stations that can be seen far out to sea stand there.
Some are so small that they are barely visible above the water,
and some are covered at high tide and then become invisible
reefs. It is these that ships have to avoid in the narrow, twisting
passages so that they do not rip open their sides on the sharp,
pointed rocks.

These islands look bleak; nevertheless, years ago people found
them and still live there. Whether they live in one of the little dells or in a minute valley where a small patch of red earth
shows, they have spent long, toilsome hours picking out every
stone from the earth. A patch not even as big as a room is already
called a "field."

With these rocks the people built stone walls around the fields
as shelter against the wind and rain that could blow or wash away
the precious earth. The walls grow layer by layer, raised higher
by each generation. They stretch themselves over the big islands

, straight, or jagged lines. At the same time
orders for adjacent pastures for goats and shee
the sparse grasses growing between juniper and
thickets and among the wild asparagus and gorse.

A few olive and fig trees always grow beside each o
tages that are scattered about the inlet. The roots gr
down between the stones to provide nourishment an
when the heat of the summer dries up the earth.

It is a poor land—rock, rock, nothing but rock. A land
out colors. For people from the north who are used
maidengreen of the spring forest, the silvery shiny olive
the cypresses dark as night do not appear very green. Thi
completely new color harmony: blue—blue in all shades,
swimming in blue. The sky above, the vast blue sea all arou
the only contrast coming from brilliant white summer clo
above and equally white rocky islands below, the white of t
islands being modified only slightly by the gray-green or blacl
green of the woods.

It is as if Nature were abundantly replacing the bleakness seen
by the naked eye. The whole land is fragrant; you can smell it
from many miles out: juniper, thyme, myrtle, rosemary!

It is a heavenly trip there between the islands with the many
large and small inlets swarming with fish. But it is most beautiful
in the wind still nights, which are uniquely animated.

From one place or another, red and white lights flash on and
off. They are the beacons that flash their warnings to the ships.
Out of the many inlets merge innumerable fishermen's boats.
Some are under sail, hauling big nets; others, sculled about almost silently by heavy steering rudders, search the water with
strong lanterns. Right at the bow a man stands carrying a many-
pronged harpoon in his hand; he watches for squid, prawns, and
whatever fish come along. As they put out to sea, the people always sing their ancient folk songs: ballads with countless verses,
wild war cries, soft, wistful love songs. Unfamiliar melodies with
drawn-out, echoing tones tell us northerners of the secret love,

sorrow, and longing of a proud nation enslaved for centuries. And although I do not understand the words, I understand the sad yearning of these men for their past. Their singing touches my heart strangely the first time I hear it. The concert of many hundreds of cicadas is like an accompaniment, and the light evening wind brings the land's fragrance—intoxicating, heavy, and sweet.

Every night spent between the islands becomes a rich, unforgettable experience for everyone.

The war broke into this peaceful world. Traveling between the islands changed overnight. Although the gentle night air is still full of the chirps of cicadas and of the heavy fragrance of the land, no one has any time to notice. The singing has become silent, for fishing is forbidden, and the men are fighting in the war.

While earlier, navigating these waters of many shoals and reefs was perilous, it has now become highly dangerous.

Mines lie between the islands. At any moment an enemy periscope, or a plane with bombs, could appear, and the nights have become exceptionally interesting; there are no more beacons! The war has extinguished them. Now we seamen must find our way about the maze of islands and tiny islands without beacons, often with overcast skies and heavy seas.

And we find help—the islands themselves offer it. Many are recognizable from a distance because of their peculiar shapes, their sharply defined silhouettes that stand out from the others at night; they make it possible for us to orient ourselves.

It is hard to believe that every island, every reef, every cliff really has its own name; however, there are some that no one forgets. Anyone who has had to prowl among them on dark nights or when there is bad weather remembers them. These are Skulj, Kurbavela, and Tetevinšnjak, before which we take off our caps in salute. These rocks and islands have often enabled our torpedo boats to find their way when the sirocco or the bora blow, and we must find our way in the night without lights![2]

That's how it had been tonight, as our boats once again came back from an uneventful expedition through the islands.

Two. U-Boats Mobilized

The torpedo boats take on coal.

Then the boat is washed with the help of steam pumps: the exterior, deck, structures, guns, and torpedo apparatus. First the boat; then the men.

Coal dust penetrates everywhere, even under the eyelids of tired eyes. We want to sleep and cannot close our eyes because they burn so much. That's why we all stand around on the dock and talk about the last trip.

The sailboats come in from the islands. Heavy, massive crafts that carry supplies, they bring sheep's cheese, fish, and schnapps, and their owners buy sugar, tobacco, and whatever else they need in town.

There is hardly any wind, and the boats must be rowed. The man sits at the helm and smokes; the women stand to row the long, heavy oars. They also moor the boat and furl the sails. It's more or less like that in the Black Mountains. When the Montenegrins come to the market at Cattaro, the man sits on the donkey; the wife runs alongside and carries the load.

One of the officers goes to see the man, who has sat down on the mooring post while the women unload the boat.

"And you? Do you do absolutely nothing whatsoever? Do you let the women do all the work?"

"Nothing? I sleep with my wife!"

But it is not as bad as it looks. All the men are fine mariners and fishermen and cultivate their land, which no farmer from the flatlands would dare to try. Their dream is to go to America where their brothers and uncle are already, to come back with a pile of dollars, and to open a restaurant.

In the evenings we officers sit in one of the two coffee houses that Sebenico boasts. It bears the impressive name, Hotel de la Ville. Greasy elegance, the floors always dirty and full of cigarette butts, the waiter in a third-hand tuxedo, with shirt and collar nearly as black. His bunions squeeze through holes cut into

Fig. 1. A torpedo boat division on a trip through the islands

someone's cast-off patent leather shoes and are polished along with the shoes!

Also, officers from the merchant ships are there. They must supply the provisions for the Gulf of Cattaro. The narrow-gauged railway cannot handle everything, and the ships that have been lying there since the beginning of the war must be supplied, as well as the military installations.

Intelligence reports come from the Bocche via cargo vessels and the incoming torpedo boats.[1] Right at the beginning of the war there had been heavy fighting there.

On top of the 1,760-meter-high Lovčen the Montenegrins had built their batteries; from there they could conveniently survey all Austrian positions.[2] They kept these positions under heavy fire daily. It was hell for our men.

Constant enemy fire hammered on their concrete bunkers, devastating them during the day. The crews would come out and patch the destroyed shelters with concrete. Day in, day out, it was like that—they did not let themselves be crushed. It was they who prevented the capture of the Bocche.

Fig. 2. A French battery shot to pieces on the Lovčen

Fig. 3. A Dalmatian sailing vessel

Fig. 4. Women "man" the fishing boats

The enemy realized all along as well as we did: the Bocche, the southernmost harbor of the monarchy, is the obvious exit of the Austro-Hungarian ships toward the Mediterranean. If the enemy succeeded in taking this harbor, then Austria would be a prisoner in the Adriatic. The Bocche is big enough to take in all the Allied ships. It would serve as a splendid harbor for the French fleet, which would then control the entire Adriatic.

For this reason it was of utmost importance to the Allies that small Montenegro be hostile to the larger Austria. Her position there above the Bocche in the Black Mountains was clearly ideal.

This was also why the French did their utmost to support Montenegro. They transported food, clothing, and munitions there. These shipments for Montenegro were accomplished with a great show of power; a major part of the French fleet had been ordered out just then to accompany the freighters to Antivari, Montenegro's only port. On these occasions, they shot constantly at coastal installations of the Bocche. They accomplished nothing, though; it seemed more like a military demonstration compared to the power at hand.

At the first appearance of the enemy fleet the small Austro-Hungarian cruiser *Zenta* was cut off by the enemy on her return to the Bocche. Seventeen big, fast, and modern warships, both English and French, had easy target practice on the small, old cruiser. The enemy ships needed only to stay out of range; the guns of the *Zenta* could not reach very far. Just one of their small, fast destroyers would have sufficed to sink the old ship.

Although her situation was hopeless, the *Zenta* defended herself furiously to the end. Everything was already destroyed; the ship was sinking, the deck awash. The commander, Captain Pachner, ordered the last salvo. The survivors thought of saving their lives only as their ship had sunk literally under their feet. But of the seventeen ships there was only one broad trail of smoke visible. The ships had left their dauntless enemy to his own devices without thinking of giving help. So the shipwrecked had to swim many miles to reach the Montenegrin coast. Enemy gunfire thinned out the rows of those exhausted to death, and when the captain finally reached the shore with the last of his men after hours of maximum exertion, he knew that a harsh imprisonment awaited them.

As a last effort to capture the Bocche, the French brought batteries to Montenegro. They pinned their highest hopes on them. The Austrian fleet waited until they had been installed on the Lovčen and then sent S.M.S. *Radetzky*. Together with the old ships that were already lying in the Gulf of Cattaro, the new batteries were bombarded and totally demolished.

Consequently the Bocche was saved and remained spared.

With the appearance of the French fleet the four Austro-Hungarian submarines that were still capable of operation were ordered down to the Bocche; more were not available. Later a fifth U-boat was added, which under the name *U-12* had fired on the French battleship *Jean Bart* near Valona and heavily damaged her.

This was the way things stood that spring evening as we officers sat together in the Hotel de la Ville in Sebenico. We discussed these and other events of the war.

In April 1915, not much was going on at the Front. We waited for something unusual, something decisive! Someone had an uncle in the ministry of war who had written very mysteriously . . . We still believed everything that came from the hinterland.

The flotilla's missions were thankless and boring: escorting cargo vessels, looking for and blowing up mines. Every now and then we had to quickly stoke up, then let the fire go out because some message about the enemy was false after all. Or we were sent out and then came back uneventfully, like this time.

"Why aren't you on a U-boat? You are an old U-boat man, aren't you?" someone asked me.

"Well, I expected this war to be quite different! I thought that on the second day after the declaration of war, we would be fighting the French in the Straits of Otranto. Was I glad I got a torpedo boat! Back then a U-boat was expected to lie in the harbor and attack the enemy only when he approached. So I wasn't very excited when they offered me a U-boat. Now, by all means, I would gladly swap."

"What kind of war is this?" grumbles another. "All the fleets lie in their harbors. The English have practically disappeared. No one knows where their fleet is. Only the small stuff is there."

"Well, what do you think?" joined in a third. "What should our and the German fleets do out there? What is the war at sea actually about? Certainly not about a cheerful little battle where we demolish each other's ships for no purpose.

"It's about control of the seas. It's about the safety of our own steamers, so we can carry on trade and safely bring back what our country needs from around the world. And this—we Central Powers can never have, because we are too weak."

Now everyone is interested in our discussion; it is obvious that this is not the first time we have debated the subject.

"Do you think Germany can so decimate the English fleet in one sea battle that she will gain the High Command of the Seas? No! No matter how many they sink, the Germans will come out so weakened that England will again rule the seas."

Obviously this would be senseless.

"And we against the French fleet? Don't even think of it. Just tell me why the fleet should put out to sea and where to! They would find no opponent out there. At best they would fall into the arms of their U-boats."

"Oh, the U-boats! They are our trump card! It's only with them that we could make it difficult for the Allies to keep command of the sea, but we'll never get it because Austria is too small."

"But then, let's move with the U-boats," I exclaim again. "Now we have finally discovered that you can shoot steamships with them; now they should be set loose like wolves on a herd!

"But the diplomats are worried. We can't sink American and Italian boats anymore; those nations could declare war. They will do that sooner or later, anyway. Yet now the English move their reinforcements under neutral flags, and our U-boats know it and have to let them go.

"We can eat cornbread but very soon this, too, will be gone. My God, haven't they caught on that this is our last chance. It's now or never!" I push back my hair excitedly and then am quiet. I let the others continue the discussion and chew on my moustache.

The officers there who know me understand how deeply I feel about U-boats.

"The German Kaiser has, however, spoken of a possible peace!" says one.

"We should be able to celebrate Christmas at home!"

"Yes, let's hope so. Waiter, my bill!"

The next morning the flotilla's flagship, the cruiser *Admiral Spaun*, hoists a signal.

"Have TB 52 get up steam by 8:00 in the evening. At 4:00 tomorrow afternoon change of command. The boat's commander is summoned."

"What can they want from me? Please, not on some big crate!"

On the flagship I receive the order. I am to hand over the torpedo boat to line officer Second Lieutenant B., and I am to proceed as a passenger on my old boat to the Gulf of Cattaro to take command of U-boat 5 there.

At first I do not know if I should be pleased.

For a long time it has been my wish to return to the U-boats, and with this I expect to encounter the enemy. But—I will be separated from my beloved division and my old torpedo boat. Once again, I must leave old friends who stood by one another so faithfully, in whose company I have spent many happy hours. Leave this crew that functions so well as a team and on whom I can depend completely.

But then, it is tempting to command a U-boat! I will be my own boss. Where there is a will, there is a way to find the enemy and perhaps do my bit to bring this accursed war to an end. The parting is brief.

"So long, have a good trip!"

The torpedo boat maneuvers around the mooring lines of her dark comrades and, with concealed lanterns, leaves port via the narrow Canal San Antonio.[3]

Relieved of my command, I go below and lie down on a berth in the officers' mess. The boat is no longer my concern.

It seems strange that the men obey another's orders: another captain will occupy this boat. Someone else will occupy my cabin, and I, like any stranger, lie in the officers' mess as a passenger.

Three. *Léon Gambetta*

S.M. torpedo boat 52 enters the Bay of Cattaro and passes by the battery of Punta d'Ostro and the island fort Mamula that guard the entrance. Both had already twice withstood the French fleet in battle. On Punta d'Ostro the artillerymen had devised an unusual defense. The batteries lie high on a sheer cliff above the sea. Below, at the base of the cliff and halfway up, they set small mines with smoky, strong gunpowder to ignite electronically.

Fig. 5. Fort Punta D'Ostro guards the entrance to the Bocche

Fig. 6. The entrance to the Bay of Cattaro

Fig. 7. The cruiser *Léon Gambetta*, 12,500 tons, 711 men

When the French fired their first rounds over the battery, the Austrians detonated the mines below to indicate too low an aim on the enemy's part. The next rounds were aimed even higher and landed far behind them in the mountains!

Through the narrow passage between the mines, the boat continues, past the launching stations, to the small harbor "Rose," which conceals the U-boats and their residence ship, the old *Crown Prince Rudolf.*[1] The torpedo boat's launch is lowered, and I take leave of my boat for the last time.

Again a new life is about to begin.

My new comrades are all familiar. Years ago, in my U-boat, I sailed with some of these men. In the meantime, some had served out their time, been home, gotten married, and now stood before me, not as young fellows, but as mature men.

"The most important thing is: we must be able to rely on one another. I must be able to trust you and you must be able to trust me, if we are to be successful and want to bring our boat back safely each time. This depends on each one of us."

My predecessor briefs me about the state of affairs in the

Fig. 8. The S.M.U. 5 is greeted by S.M.S. *Monarch*

Bocche. The news is not very encouraging. Of the seven U-boats that the navy possesses, four are stationed in the Gulf of Cattaro. Two are needed to protect Trieste; these are worthless and good for only very short trips. The seventh lies in Pola. All the boats are old, and they have a lot of mechanical problems and little possibility of repair since there is no quality repair shop available. Although the war has already been going on for nine months, the conditions are primitive and makeshift. All repairs are made with materials at hand, and the men work day and night in order to keep the boats halfway ready for war. They have to economize with everything, and the High Command seems to have no understanding of their needs.

"We have to be self-sufficient if we want to sail at all," my predecessor says. "Have you seen our motor boat? Even old Noah would have had problems with it! The glorious Navy does not care enough about us. We are the neglected stepchildren everywhere and first need to assert ourselves. Up until recently, we weren't even allowed to test our torpedoes by ourselves! Those in the arsenal took care of that; they should be able to do a better job! But even there the torpedoes seem to have been sabotaged. The result was that our torpedoes ran crooked."

The men are first rate, clever, and willing. Give them an empty sardine can and they will make you a carburetor. I wonder only how they have kept up their enthusiasm. They, too, need success for a change!

Nothing has been seen of the enemy for a long time. Since *U-12* torpedoed the French flagship *Jean Barth*, the Adriatic has been empty of warships. Occasionally we can capture a few small coastal vessels; at night they want to smuggle their shipments from San Giovanni di Medua toward Montenegro, but the neutral cargo vessels of the Puglia line that supply Montenegro through Albania are "taboo."

I feel hot resentment rising slowly.

"We are such fools," I tell the man who is orienting me. "We hold ourselves scrupulously to the international regulations of the right of capture and the raiding of ships.[2] The enemy must be amazed at how well-behaved we are. He certainly has it easy: supply Montenegro through neutral cargo ships that have been cleared for neutral Albania. Everyone knows that the merchandise is brought over from there to Montenegro, and we let these transports run by in front of our noses and are not allowed to take them!"

"Yes," says the other, "their captains salute ours sarcastically, and we must make the best of it." Sure enough, the next day I receive orders from the admirals to adhere strictly to the international regulations.

Since neither war nor merchant ships are in the Adriatic, I must go hunting in another region. A cruiser has been reported in the Strait of Otranto every now and then. She is supposed to cut off the Adriatic from the world and prevent the Austrian fleet from breaking unseen into the Mediterranean. So far the flotillas have been unable to find this cruiser; however, she appears in the Strait of Otranto every now and then. Moreover, it has been reported that the French fleet has hidden itself away in Astacco, a harbor on the Greek coast by Santa Maura, which must have escaped the Greek government completely.

With their small cruising radius, the U-boats can go just about that far.

Two days later at 4:00 in the morning, *U-5* silently undoes her moorings. We want to be out of sight of land by daybreak because the Montenegrins can look out from Lovčen at the whole Bocche and keep sight of a departing boat for a long time. Their radio station could inform the enemy of an approaching U-boat, and that would not be what we need.

On the *Rudolf* everyone is still asleep except the watch, who calls after the boat, "Have a good trip!"

Hugging the coast, our course skirts our own mines. We flash the identifying signal to the forts and shore batteries, and soon our boat reaches free, navigable water.

The sirocco drives rainsqualls ahead of itself as it advances. It is wet and cold and the atmosphere feels unfriendly and chilly. Slowly pressing on, the boat works against the seas with difficulty; they inundate her on and off, part at the conning tower, and then run like a waterfall to either side.[3]

The regular beat of one laboring engine can be heard up here, and we on watch keep peering down the conning tower, waiting for the hot tea that would cheer us up.

Except for us, everyone has disappeared below. The crew worked up to the moment they had put out to sea to get the boat and engine ready, and now each one is catching up on as much sleep as he can.

With the rising sun, the wind turns to south-southeast, the rain showers slowly break off, and the clouds clear.

With daylight, rain gear is removed and the lookouts stretch comfortably on the conning tower in the warm sun.

The colors of the high black mountains of Montenegro and the Krivošije blend with the dark shades of the clouds that cannot find their way out of the mountains. The land disappears, and the last link with the homeland is lost.

"Sir, I must call your attention to something. The boat is old and worn out. We have tried again and again, but it is impossible to get the engines tight, and exhaust and gas fumes come into the boat. For example, if we submerge now without ventilating the boat ahead of time, in an hour half the crew will be unconscious. Men will fall like flies, and we will be able to revive them only after we surface and bring them into fresh air.

"But the crew doesn't seem to mind. They call this condition 'gasoline stupor' and laugh about it. But at some point it could become dangerous. We definitely need other engines, diesel engines that run with oil, not these old gas motors."

"Well," I answer, "we cannot do much about that. The boats are all needed. As long as we have so few U-boats, we cannot think of installing new engines. It would be too time-consuming. We can't do without a single boat and must get as much as possible out of each one. It is a real shame that we have such junk to work with."

In the evening light, signals from the Italian coast come in sight. The course is ten miles from land toward the south. I tell the crew the situation. For hours binoculars stare into the darkness and look on all sides for the blockade cruiser that is supposedly there. Everyone's eyes tire and see things that are not there: once a light, then a dark shadow, and again and again, it was an illusion.

Wait a minute, there is something! A dark spot on the dark water. He who saw it first whispers to his neighbor. He does not want to cause unnecessary alarm. It is unquestionably a ship. The boat comes about and it becomes evident: a gaff-rigged schooner that slowly steers in the direction of the Italian coast. We two officers confer. A boat search is pointless. At best we would give ourselves away and the big prey would be lost. We let him go.

The next morning finds our boat in the latitude of Corfu. We continue on a southerly course because I hope to find something near Ithaca. All the ships going to Astacco have to pass by there.

The feeble wind slackens and the sea becomes as glassy as a mirror.

A small bird flutters around the boat and alights exhausted on deck. Men scatter breadcrumbs his way, but he doesn't eat. He is just dead-tired. I remember my first trip on a sailboat in the Mediterranean. It was in the fall when migratory birds travel south. One morning the rigging was full of hawks. They sat together on the lines and spreaders, so tired that we could catch them with our bare hands. After a couple of hours, they moved on.

"Smoke aft of starboard!"

The cry is spread in the boat; in no time everyone is on his feet and on deck. Far beyond the horizon, so that it hardly stands out from the sky, a fine streak of smoke drags toward the south. Far off course. Our boat travels at full power to intercept the ship's path. Submerged, she would travel too slowly; she must try to get ahead of the ship's course above water as closely as possible. Soon the tops of the masts appear above the horizon and climb higher out of the water. The ship is approaching much too fast. You can already see the tops of the stacks; soon, the bridge will rise from the horizon. It is high time to dive before we are sighted.

The men disappear rapidly through the tower hatch; one of them quickly snatches the bird and takes it along. There isn't enough time to properly ventilate the boat's interior. The flood-valves are opened and water rushes into the ballast tanks to make U-5 heavier so she can dive. I disappear last into the conning tower, closing the hatch behind me. With the bow leading the way, the boat dives into the deep. The pounding of the engines has given way to the light hum of the electric motors. The men stand at their battle stations. The torpedoes are prepared forward and the chief engineer regulates the balance and trim of the boat with the pump.

After that everything is absolutely still.

From my place at the periscope I can overlook the whole boat. The torpedo apparatus is forward, aft the engines, to the left the driving rudder and the valves for the different tanks. The periscope is my biggest concern. To be sure, with an improvised arrangement, I can raise and lower it, but that goes so slowly that it is easier to steer the whole boat higher or deeper so as to look out of the water with the periscope or to submerge it. You cannot really approach a ship and watch it through the periscope. You can only observe it from time to time because the wake from the periscope betrays the submarine's presence and the ship under attack only needs to turn its rudder a small amount to avoid the attack. Besides, the sea is so smooth today it would be a miracle if we were not detected.

Finally our boat is close enough to the oncoming ship that our speed can be decreased. We bring out the ship register. French, of the model *Victor Hugo*. I rarely need the periscope. The man on the diving rudder has to work hard.

Once more the periscope breaks through the water's surface. The cruiser that was earlier to port is now to starboard. Our boat comes about. By the next lookout, it is clear: we have been discovered. The cruiser runs in a large circle around us and then goes on its original course toward Cape Ducato.

"Do you know what we saw tonight?" I let slip. "That was the cruiser! She has one group of stacks forward, the second aft, and those were the alleged gaff sails. Nothing else. Confound it! And tonight we could have sunk her so beautifully!"

I leave the periscope free for the men to look through. One after another they look through it. Now there is nothing left to ruin.

I feel foolish. During the night the enemy ran right into my arms, but I let him escape. During the day I betrayed myself and was discovered. But at least I have found this out: the blockade cruiser is not on the alert at night. In the darkness he appears to feel safe from our U-boat. So he will probably come again. I need only patience and endurance.

The men lie around the boat apathetically. The beginnings of "gasoline stupor" have started, and everyone has a headache. With the first fresh air after surfacing, the crew returns to life.

Our boat lies near the Italian coast and the lighthouse from Cape Santa Maria de Leuca flashes its light across to us.

The engines are stopped, and absolute quiet reigns. Fore and aft a few men sit and dangle their feet in the water. From below waft the sounds of a harmonica that apparently changes hands as the melodies change from German to Hungarian to Italian, then to Slavic. Just a piece of the Austrian empire, crowded together into a tiny space.

In one corner, engine mate Hermann writes in a notebook. He, too, wants to record something of this "important time" for posterity. Another reads through his last letters once more.

Also the cook has been reactivated. Now that we are all well again, we want food ready to eat! The "life line," as the men call it, is canned meat that came from the French U-boat *Marie Curie* that was captured in the antisubmarine nets off Pola. Mixed with potatoes it makes a delicious goulash.

In the night "she" is there again. Just like an old friend who shows up for the rendezvous. She stands out easily against the moon. I plot my course so I can fire above water. Everything is ready and in a couple of minutes I must fire. At that point the cruiser comes about unexpectedly and takes off at full steam. Our U-boat is now behind her and an attempt to gain on her fails once more. The cruiser is moving too fast.

Everyone in the boat is indignant: surely the enemy had definite orders to patrol until sunrise and now, at 2:00 in the morning, she is heading back. Such dereliction of duty!

The following day the torpedoes are taken out of their tubes and lubricated, the steering mechanism is tested, and the compressed air, which drives them, is repumped. The accumulator batteries are recharged.

If only the day would pass quickly.

This is the last night that our boat can stay out. The fuel is running out.

I study my charts and calculate with compass and triangle. During these two days I have learned several bits of information about this nocturnal cruiser, but my calculations are still an equation with many unknowns. Consider this: the enemy advances from the southeast, in which case she will be visible against the bright moon. Ten nautical miles from land she takes up his post, cruising back and forth—slowly, to make as little smoke as possible. She has done this these past few nights. Our U-boat must hide out in the land's shadow in order to let the cruiser come near with the moon behind her. Then later the cruiser should steer out to sea and continue slowly southward, anticipating the moon's westward course toward land. After midnight, the cruiser will head back to her base.

Yes, it must happen that way. The watch officer agrees with me.

Yet you cannot force this to happen.

Everything proceeds as planned. The moon rises and its silver gleam lies bright on the water's lightly agitated surface. No ship can avoid being spotted against this brightness in its course.

Those men off duty sleep with one eye open, but they don't get any rest. Anticipation will not permit sleep.

I consider how I should carry out the attack. I could be discovered all too soon above water; also I have no sighting device. I must aim with the boat itself and, calculating the enemy's speed, figure out an angle in front of the cruiser. Such a visual estimate would not be accurate to the exact degree, so, I will try to torpedo the enemy from a submerged position and hope that the moon will send enough light through the periscope.

An underwater attack at night has never been attempted in the U-boat branch of the service, neither in peacetime nor in war. But I want to risk it; it appears a sure success.

Toward midnight there is a general alert. The dark shadow of the cruiser rises distinctly against the moon in my binoculars. No light is visible on board. Smokeless and calm, the enemy moves slowly northward, as though everyone on board were sleeping. Still, dozens of pairs of eyes must be straining to look out into the night.

Soundlessly our U-boat steers toward our adversary until she can be seen with the naked eye; then she continues underwater.

At first I cannot find the ship in the periscope. I get worried: would I be able to discern the cruiser in the periscope? Would the moon give enough light?

I look and look but can see nothing.

By now, the enemy could have changed course.

The men are completely disheartened. To them my command "dive" was synonymous to "we are letting him go." They had never before heard of an underwater attack at night.

I am unaware of their bitter disappointment. For me these are painful minutes. Will I let the opportunity slip by for the fourth time? There—as a minute speck—I discover the ship again. I heave a sigh of relief. I let the men standing around me look through the periscope quickly. Then I need it back for myself.

Without a word the men understand: we are attacking! Fatigue and depression vanish. With utmost concentration they watch my facial expressions. My pantomime is the sole reflection of what is about to happen on the surface in the silent moonlit night above.

The cruiser comes about. If she veers away, everything is in vain again. But this time she approaches our U-boat. Slowly the picture in the periscope grows. I think I hear the rushing of the bow wake as the colossus moves closer. Now a quick glance at the ship type; there is no doubt, again a *Victor Hugo*.

"Both torpedoes ready!"—and the last safety device of the projectiles is unfastened, and . . . "ready!" comes back. In the periscope I can see the cruiser's bow run through the crosshairs of the ocular, then the forward tower, the command bridge. Now the aft stacks come, with the most vital part of the ship, the boilers.

"Starboard torpedo—fire!" then a quick turn and "Port torpedo—fire!" toward the forward stacks. I watch the trail of air bubbles from my projectiles. They run in a straight line at 40 knots to their targets. At 500 meters' distance a big ship can no longer evade them.

There—a dull, hard sound, after ten seconds a second one, as if a knuckle hit an iron plate, and a cloud of smoke shoots high up, far above the topmasts.

The men in the boat cannot hold back. "Hurrah! Hurrah!" and again "Hurrah!" Somehow or other they must release the tension. I have difficulty penetrating their enthusiasm to get them to ready the reserve torpedoes. Perhaps the ship still requires a coup de grâce.

Aft of the mortally wounded enemy, our U-boat crosses her course. The ship lists heavily on her port side and tries to put out lifeboats. A terrible state of affairs must be prevalent on board. The electric generators have stopped and the ship is completely dark. In the sudden sinister darkness down below, surely no one can find the closed bulkhead doors. The invading water, the slanting decks, the suddenly sloping ladders, the boiler's explosion—all that must spread confusion and mortal terror. No boats can be put out from the starboard side because the ship lists too much to port.

Everything happens very quickly. The thin silhouette in the periscope becomes noticeably smaller, only a thin streak is visible and then it, too, disappears. Nine minutes after firing.

Our U-boat surfaces.

I quickly scan the horizon. Is there absolutely no escort ship? Did they let the ship travel all alone? Without a destroyer? Without a torpedo boat? No, there is nothing in sight; only five lifeboats adrift in the water. One of them has a light. Hats off to the French who brought so many safely into the water.

"Seyffertitz, now that's a nice kettle of fish!" I murmur to my second officer. "What shall we do about these Frenchmen? Couldn't they bring one single vessel along? How are we supposed to help now? Such carelessness!"

We two officers discuss the situation with each other. We cannot take any more men in the U-boat. It can tolerate no excess weight when submerging and resurfacing. The Frenchmen could not stay on deck either. Whenever our boat would have to dive, they would have to swim; thus, they were safer in their own boats. Anyway, there couldn't be many survivors.

With a heavy heart, I order the engines to be turned on, and I set a course for the Gulf of Cattaro.

"They let our men from the *Zenta* drown, too," I hear one of the men say.

The man is right, but I cannot bear to hear that yet. With a sudden movement I turn away. I feel a choking in my throat. I want to be alone.

I feel as if something were strangling me. Exhausted, I lean against the conning tower and stare with fatigued eyes toward the shrinking dots . . . the boats I cannot help.

So that's what war looks like! There behind me hundreds of seamen have drowned, men who have done me no harm, men who did their duty as I myself have done, against whom I have nothing personally; with whom, on the contrary, I have felt a bond through sharing the same profession. Approximately seven hundred men must have sunk with the ship!

In the beginning it had been like a peacetime maneuver; the days of searching, then once, twice, three times a failed opportunity . . . the enormous tension: will we ever get him? All this obscured the seriousness of the situation.

Now the tension is gone. We got him.

Suddenly I notice how little we have slept in the last few days, never longer than three hours; in addition, there were the toxic fumes in the boat—everything has worn out my nerves. I feel something hot and angry rise up inside. I turn to my second-in-command:

"Say Seyffertitz, our job is horrible! We are like highwaymen, sneaking up on an unsuspecting ship in such a cowardly fashion. At least if we were in the trenches or on a torpedo boat, that would be something else! There you hear shooting, near you comrades fall, you hear the wounded groaning—you become filled with rage and can shoot men in self defense or fear; at an assault you can even yell! But we! Simply cold-blooded to drown a mass of men in an ambush!"

"Yes sir!"

ur 'yes sir!' Don't sleep; say something!"

nt. But there is more to our trade than to

or on a torpedo boat. I think it takes more

ave it better than the men and me. We know

about what is going on up there. We can see

know that you are going for an attack. You have no time to talk, but we must read your facial expressions and infer what is going on up there."

I listen to him. I have never really thought about it that way. I tear my eyes away from the sea and look squarely at him, as he carries on:

"What—treachery? Couldn't we be torpedoed at any moment or run into mine fields? They have laid nets against U-boats in the English Channel. Supposedly they have sound apparatus to detect us. You know, they are going to invent all sorts of things to make life tougher for us. We are not just a 'glory weapon.'"

"You're right, Seyffertitz. Where are the days when an old sailboat captain would pass his enemy at a couple of cables' lengths and greet his enemy from the poop deck? 'A vous le premier coup!' When chivalry was still in control of all warfare. Those days are gone. The last knight, though, is our old Emperor, who, after the declaration of war, sent the Serbian chief of the general staff Putnik home in a Pullman car, instead of taking him prisoner. Against the statesmen, who work with defamations of character, who twist international agreements, and who terrorize neutral countries . . . compared to those, a U-boat is a pretty respectable guy!"

Slowly the stars fade. The moon has already long gone down and dawn begins to break.

Silently we stand, commander, watch officer, and a couple of men at the conning tower. Sleep is out of the question, although all of us are dog-tired. The cook sends up scrambled eggs; no one can eat. We can only smoke, and schnapps helps.

The oldest petty officer comes up to congratulate me. Little by little those off duty show up on deck. They stand a tower in groups and whisper.

One comes forward:

"Sir, will we receive medals for bravery?"

Right, that will probably happen. So there is another side to this situation.

What will the people back home say? This is the first sunk warship for us! Our boat will be greeted with cheers and on land we will have a look at the medals for bravery. All at once the trip passes too slowly.

By noon the mountains of home are already in sight. But the coast does not get nearer. The trip stretches terribly.

One man shaves; then the other ones dress up, too.

Torpedo master Valašek takes photographs. He fired the torpedoes.

In time the coast comes into view; then our boat goes around the mines in front of the harbor entrance, and with the last light of the setting sun, we take our mooring in Rose.

From the residence ship, the old *Crown Prince Rudolf*, we are questioned.

"Hello, what's new?"

"Sank a French cruiser."

"Bravo! So it was you. The news was telegraphed here. Do you know her name?"

"No!"

"It was the *Léon Gambetta*!"[4]

Four. Letters

"So Seyffertitz, the seriousness of life begins. Now the hardest part for me comes—the endless paperwork! Tomorrow you square away the boat until it shines."

On the *Crown Prince Rudolf*, the men line the rails and wait for the arrival of *U-5*. The news of the sinking has already come via Italy. Italian torpedo boats had saved the shipwrecked survivors and had brought them to land. Nearly the entire staff of officers had gone down with the ship so that the crew could be saved in the lifeboats.

Everyone here congratulates me.

"Let me go! I still have to report this; the Admiral will want to know something, too!"

I connect with the flagship by telephone. "This is the commander of *U-5*. Can I speak with the chief of staff?"

"He is eating at the Admiral's and cannot come to the telephone."

"Well, they are not exactly curious," I comment to those standing near me; I leave a short message. Then I enter the officers' mess and we from *U-5* must recount the whole event with great precision. After all, these are specialists who want to know the smallest detail. Our friends' pure delight about the success of our boat is heartwarming. We celebrate the event and, overtired, we get to sleep only late at night.

The next morning, per the Admiral's orders, *U-5* goes around the whole fleet division lying in the Gulf and is greeted joyfully by all ships and boats with cries of "Hurrah!" On the flagship the band is playing the Radetzky March and the Prince Eugene March, and our boat's crew becomes conscious that they, for the first time, are "somebody." At least for today.

Our boat comes alongside the flagship to recharge her batteries. On board we are congratulated and must retell the story again. Also telegrams have come in from all possible quarters. Now begins the hard work of writing. Letters and parcels arrive and we men of *U-5* swim in champagne and Dalmatian wine.

Here are two of the letters:

"To His Imperial Royal Highness, the Captain of the *U-5*"

The great heroic deed that our sailors performed cannot be described. With iron diligence, bravery, and valor they fight for an upright, peaceful Austria. Under your imperial and royal command, the biggest French cruiser was sunk. We congratulate the great heroic exploit of the submarine *U-5* with the wish that the victory banners of the submarines will flutter in the city of Vienna.

With God for Emperor and fatherland, every hand is raised in Austria.

Yours respectfully,
Your once again well-wishing
Viennese friend
An eighth grade schoolgirl[1]
Vienna XI Enkplatz 4.

So the womenfolk are beginning, too. I am touched and order a *Prügelkrapfen* from the confectioner Lehmann of Singerstrasse to be delivered to the girl.[2] The outcome of all this is unexpected. Suddenly it seems all the Viennese schoolgirls have gotten a writing bug because it rains little letters from schoolgirls who are sooo happy and so on. But such a *Prügelkrapfen* is expensive and, at the moment, I don't have time to open a bakery myself.

So many letters arrive that a couple of friends take pity on me and help with the replies. But one letter sets me thinking. An old school friend whose father came from Hannover around 1866 and had made it to K.u.K. army colonel sent it.[3] The writer himself had become an Austrian officer but had to leave the military on account of illness and had lived for years in Germany. The letter reads:

May 1, 1915
Dear Georg,

. . . For four days all the newspapers have carried your name throughout the world and you have climbed several rungs higher on the ladder to world fame. I hope to God you will be preserved for the fatherland for a long time because Austria especially needs real men, for she has enough womenfolk.

For me your courageous feat is an especial joy in the thought of the bitter disappointment that your colleagues in the army daily hand our troops who are fighting with them. All the newspapers' gossip cannot obscure the facts, and only since Hindenburg re-grouped the various troops, do the "born losers," as we call your colleagues here, have someone to give them some backbone. Single brave deeds still occur, of course, among them, but the average is really only good enough for a tragedy. From a military standpoint our leaders unanimously believe that it must be pure joy for the enemy to wage war against these "born losers." Well, politics have brought us together by fate and here [in Germany] no one doubts a final victory. After peacetime, may German strength also come to the Danube and make impossible for all time repetitions of the shameful invasion of Serbia and the scandalously poor provisions at Pryzemysl. My brother is keeping an eye on the Italians for whom you, if God so wills, can prepare another Lissa if need be.[4] In spite of all the loud rumors, nobody believes that they can cause us serious damage.

Where in the world will my letter reach you!

Hip, hip hurrah!

Your old N. N.

I feel sick at heart. So that is how they talk about Austria over there? After Austria's army bled to death holding up the Russian Steamroller? Six months after the breakdown on the Marne. After the heavy Austrian mortars had helped to conquer the Belgian strongholds.

Why all this? Is there a hidden intent?

Five. Envy

U-5 steers toward the Drin Gulf. Calm weather, bright moonlit night, the second officer, the torpedo master, and a lookout are on guard. I sleep on the floor of the boat. One man awakens me: "The lieutenant asks you to please come on deck."

"Is something in sight?"

"No sir, but the torpedo master is acting so peculiarly."

"I will be right there." I wipe the sleep from my eyes and go up. A couple of officers are talking in whispers.

"Sir, the torpedo master is crazy. He sees the French fleet everywhere, once to starboard, then from all sides. In the moonbeams he sees dead Frenchmen swimming in the water who wave at him. He calls, 'Emergency dive!' and wants to go below and tear open the flood valves. Apparently he is paranoid."

"Hmmm. We have to do something. He could really be dangerous, poor fellow. Do we have any schnapps on board?"

"Yes, in the medicine cabinet."

"Have someone relieve him from his watch and send him to me below!"

I invite him for a tumbler of Cognac and ask him if he wouldn't like to go home on leave. He has been on board so long and needs a break. His folks at home haven't seen him with the medal for valor. At first the petty officer fidgets in his chair, again and again he seems drawn to the nearest flood valve, and the tanks of compressed air are attractive to him. I inquire about his family, give him another glass of cognac, and with time, the man calms down and becomes drowsy.

Then a petty officer relieves me, takes over the role of watching the one resting, and must not let him out of his sight.

"He is too weird for me; he could do us all sorts of harm out of fear. Regular war psychosis. We are going home. We cannot watch over him days on end. Too bad; such a fine, honest fellow."

Then I lie down on my hard bed.

The next morning the boat is located outside the southern-most mine passage of the Bocche. A torpedo boat arrives from the North and behind her still another vessel. Both U-boat officers are on deck and keep their eyes on the arrivals.

"What is that over there behind the torpedo boats? It looks like a U-boat but they don't come that big. Have they actually captured an English warship?"

"Isn't it a type made by the Germania shipyards? But so big."

The two are unsure until they can make out the flags in our binoculars.

"Oho, German war flags. How did they get here?"

U-5 travels at full speed to reach the German, but cannot make any headway against her speed. Like a small puppy that cannot keep up with its master.

For the arrival the torpedo master is permitted on deck. He sits forward and smiles happily to himself, since he knows he is in a safe harbor. He looks a bit bleary-eyed after all that alcohol. Everyone says a friendly word to him and he looks forward to this promised leave of absence.

The goal of *U-5* is S.M.S. *Gäa*, that functions as torpedo mother ship. The German U-boat lies alongside the steamship and *U-5* moors in front of her to recharge her batteries.

On the deck of the *Gäa* the railing is densely occupied. Everyone wants to examine the monster of a U-boat.

She has an enormous conning tower, with large safety walls behind which you can stay dry in the heaviest weather. Two periscopes and an 8.8-centimeter gun. You could shoot at a cargo vessel with it. You can see by looking at it that the boat has just completed a long sea voyage. For eighteen days they were en route around England, and what is most impressive, they were able to accomplish the whole long trip with their original fuel supply.

I go on board the German ship and welcome the commander of *U-21*, Lieutenant Hersing, who at this time had sunk the *Pathfinder*, an English cruiser—the first warship of this war to be sunk in the North Sea. I am welcomed very cordially and go through the boat, at least to get a cursory impression.

What this boat has is unbelievable! Powerful diesel, the engine room separated from the other parts by bulkheads; on the whole, the boat is divided into many compartments. One large control room to handle the diving maneuver, a spacious conning tower, two periscopes that are electrically raised or lowered. The U-boat needs only to be taken down to the desired depth; the periscope takes care of the lookout on its own. Torpedo shafts fore and aft. The men have proper berths, the commander even an honest-to-goodness cabin with an electric lamp next to his bed. A dining table for the officers and a mess table for the crew. Like a luxury steamer compared to my old boat. Construction for air recycling, a separate radio cubicle. It is like being in Wonderland and the Germans are not even aware of it. They act as if this were commonplace. Fierce envy overcomes me. Next to the other boat I feel ashamed as an Austrian officer. With difficulty, I invite Hersing to visit.

Nevertheless, I do it. There is not much to explain. With one glance a U-boat man can comprehend the whole room. Hersing looks around:

"I would refuse to travel in this crate."

Six. Trip to the Hinterland

Additional German U-boats have come into the Bocche. Fine chaps who had already sunk many tons around England and en route to the Mediterranean.

Those from the North have to get used to our Austrian German at first. They also have different expressions that we soon easily understand. They have lots to tell and it is a happy gathering.

While all this is happening, I receive the news that my brother, an army captain, has been killed in action in Galicia.

Two days later I am sitting on the train with my wife on the way to Innsbruck to fetch my brother's widow, who has no relatives in Austria.[1] We are bringing her to live with our family. She had married shortly before the war and, with her small child, was practically foreign in the country.

The lunch stop is in Wörgl, and you must cross the street to get to the inn. On the way I meet a dignified gentleman in a Red Cross uniform who asks me if he might have the honor of shaking my hand.

"Hello, now you've got it. What do you say in a situation like this?" I think to myself as I shake hands with him and stammer a few friendly words. Then quickly back into the railroad car to avoid another encounter. On the platform a row of people stand waving their hats and calling, "Heil!"

"*Himmelblauer Höllteufel,* now we must go receive their congratulations," I remark in an aside to my wife; I grin in a friendly manner and greet the delighted well-wishers.[2] Then I take refuge in my compartment and want to close the curtains, but these had been stolen long ago.

"I will have to learn the mannerisms of an arch-duke if this continues." Then the train finally leaves.

In Innsbruck we fetch our sister-in-law and take her back the following day. When I ask for the bill at the hotel Tiroler Hof, the innkeeper considers it an honor to put us up as guests.

At the train station the white-clothed waiters step up, call "Heil!" and draw attention to me. A couple of my brother's friends and comrades greet us and help me stow both women and the child on the train, helping me out of my embarrassment.

The trip to the dining car becomes a virtual hurdle race. At every door at least one well-wisher stands with the weekly newspaper in hand, wanting to have an autograph beneath my picture.

Finally I can get off the train in Zell am See; I have already learned to greet people very graciously. The next day as I travel on to Vienna, I am in civilian clothes. There, at the naval office,

I receive orders to deliver His Majesty's orders verbally to the Division's commander in the Bocche.

Italy's declaration of war is expected at any time, and the order cannot be given in writing. In the evening the train leaves Vienna from the South Station. It is a long trip to Castelnuovo, the terminus of the Bosnian railway, and I intend to put to sea immediately upon arrival. I want to arrive well rested. My orders are made out for second class, but that is constantly overcrowded. I take out the paper, make a thick 1 out of the 2 and ask for my ticket.

"Please, sir, are the instructions made out for first or second class? I cannot read it," asks the official.

"Look, that was a two, and I have made a one over it. I want to be able to sleep."

"But you cannot do that. . . . Well, I will stick my neck out for you," and the official gives me a first class ticket. I thank him and am asleep in a first class bunk as the train leaves the station.

Near Baden I am rudely awakened. A forefinger bores its way in my ribs one after the other, and a harsh voice resounds.

"Ticket collector. Ticket please."

The only people that I loathe are the ticket collector and the dining car waiter. The first drills you awake with his fingers; the other shouts so long until you wake up. I look angrily for my ticket; the controller studies it for a long time and then says indignantly, "The order really says second class."

"Yes, yes, but not any more. Don't you see that I made a one out of it?" I roll over and try not to lose my sleep altogether. The ticket collector speaks again, then grumbles helplessly and disappears.

The next afternoon I find myself with an army captain on his trip to Bosnia-Brod. The train is two hours late and it is doubtful I will make the connection for Bosnia.

"If you are a courier, you need only to telegraph as a courier from the next station to Bosnia Brod. Then they have to wait."

In the next station I telegraph and as the train enters Bosnia-Brod, my name is called out and a friendly station master informs me that the train has waited, a compartment is reserved, and over there is the refreshment room for possible refreshment. That is somewhat different from the Southern Railway's conductor, I think as I thank him. I stick a bottle of mineral water under my arm and sit in my compartment. I make myself comfortable there and sleep until five o'clock in the morning.

I could have slept longer, but the conductor informs me that a young lady would like to speak with me.

"A young lady? I don't know any young ladies in all of Bosnia. I will come right out, but first let me put on my trousers."

With a handful of mineral water I wet my face, go through my hair with my fingers, and then I am ready for the lady's visit. A dear young girl stands on the platform and, blushing, presents me with a huge bouquet of flowers. A dozen freshly picked fragrant roses. I would like to give her a kiss, but a crowd of people is standing around and I do not want to make the little one more embarrassed.

This continues at all the stations. Flowers, always flowers, and I yearn for a cup of coffee and a slice of bread and butter. In Sarajevo the mayor and his family greet me. Are there only pretty girls in Bosnia? But it seems a mother-in-law is with them, too. I have lunch with them.

From Mostar onward I can finish the trip by car. Supposedly Italy has declared war and this makes me hurry to my boat.

Seven. The Bomb Exploded

News of Italy's declaration of war is confirmed. I am not surprised. On the contrary, everyone in the navy has expected it since the beginning of the war. Everyone knows that the Italian border is unprotected. Until the necessary troops are taken from other scenes of action to build a new Italian front, all Istria, and with it, Pola, the chief war harbor, could be cut off from the interior by an unexpected advance from Italy. The land fortifications of Pola are ancient and would be no serious hindrance to the enemy; they could be overrun in the first assault.

So there is a danger that the central headquarters of the navy with its arsenals, resources, equipment, and coal could be lost. If that happened, the activity of the whole fleet could be undermined.

At this point the fleet itself makes a move.

At 4:00 p.m. on the twenty-third of May, Italy's declaration of war is known in Pola and three hours later the entire Austrian fleet leaves port. In groups they spread out along the east coast of Italy, from Ravenna down to Barletta, and they shoot at the railway and at whatever military installations they can find.

In a fight between destroyers, the Italian *Turbine* is sunk.

The surprise attack has the desired effect: the Italians' advance toward the Isonzo is delayed.[1] Perhaps a landing maneuver is expected on the other side. At any rate, time is gained, the Isonzo front is established, and the danger for Pola is dispelled.

For now the U-boats are held back and are used only on the home coast. Two lie in Trieste, one in Pola, one in Lissa, and the rest in the Bocche.

Everyone awaits an offensive action from the Italians and wants to have the U-boats on hand.

Naturally, with these few the whole coast cannot be defended and so around and among the islands, enemy U-boats make themselves apparent. Otherwise, at present, the enemy is not noticeable.

Eight. **Poor Austrians!**

Meanwhile, the German U-boats conduct economic warfare in the Mediterranean and sink freighters.

One after the other!

And it is so simple: they lie on a steamship route and do not have to look long. The ships come on the shortest route between the harbors. Each alone, one after the other!

As soon as a freighter draws near, the U-boat surfaces and flies the signal: "Stop immediately!"

Then the captain is called down below with his papers. Most transports have contraband goods—and then the demolition squad goes on board.

Our route first leads us to the supply compartments, since the ships always bring the most delicious things home: canned food, caviar, wines, cognac, whole sides of bacon, but also chronometers and sextants. It would be a pity to sink all these lovely goods.

Then blasting cartridges are let down on the ship's hull, detonated, and the ship has made her last voyage.

Sometimes these ships follow one another so quickly that the first has not yet sunk before the next in line appears.

Many stop even without summons and the crew rushes into the lifeboats, their respect for the U-boats is so great. However, should one attempt to escape, the 8.8-centimeter cannon quickly brings her surrender.

Some good-natured commanders are willing to tow the lifeboats with the shipwrecked sailors to the coast and then move on to the next cargo vessel.

Now and then the Germans bring home another variety of loot. One comes with a small cannon, one with a lot of copper that was really needed for the production of ammunition, and one brings a black man. They had fished him out of a sinking cargo ship where the man had been abandoned. Later he answers to the name, "Wilhelm," and is quite a skillful fellow. When tobacco is scarcest, he sells his masters good cigarettes that he had stolen from them the week before.

Max Valentiner even brings back a camel from the North African coast, a gift from the Senussi. He had brought Turkish officers there who, equipped with money and medals, were to agitate the different clans against the English and the Italians. According to the German officers' story, these emissaries decorated one another with the highest medals of distinction and divided the money amongst themselves until Valentiner intervened strongly.

The K.u.K. U-boats have similar, although shorter, expeditions to carry out. Again and again an Albanian chieftain comes on board who, furnished with coffers of gold and weapons, should be deposited in the Drin Gulf on land. You retreat instinctively before them. Unshaved and unwashed, with matted hair, they look like the last survivors of a polar expedition. They just don't look like chiefs at all. Instead, they reek from a distance. They are also suspected of having brought the first bedbugs on board the U-boats.

They are naturally very influential, high-ranking dignitaries and promise to call Albania to arms against Italy . . .

The U-boat men are sorry about the lovely gold. How many good German periscopes can be bought for that?

But this pleasant steamship war does not last long. A U-boat brings home the news that steamers are now being armed. Only after a long gunfight did they succeed in sinking a steamer.

At first the ships have only small cannons aft, but with time they get bigger and soon can defend themselves successfully against the U-boats with large caliber cannons.

This is something completely new! An armed merchant ship, even when it flies commercial colors, must be regarded as a warship—and a warship can be sunk without warning from underwater.

The English have thought up something else: they travel under neutral, thus false, colors.

And then we hear for the first time about U-boat traps. These English vessels have camouflaged guns on board and they pretend to be tramp steamers. When such a ship is stopped, it blows off steam, and waits until a U-boat comes near. Then suddenly the disguise drops away from the machine guns, which open fierce gunfire on the surprised U-boat.

But the Austrian U-boats cannot keep pace with the Germans. Their fuel supply does not permit such long voyages. Instead, they lie in wait off the Albanian coast in front of Brindisi as well as between the native islands, and they scour the Strait of Otranto. It is hardly worth the trouble.

Five brand new submarines lie in the Germania shipyard in Kiel under construction for the Austro-Hungarian navy, the outcome of the experiments made with the first trial boats. They were the hope of the old U-boat men. But the boats have already been sold to the Germans, as if the K.u.K. fleet had no enemies in the North Sea. They could also have been brought over here . . .

It is best not to discuss the matter with those who had a part in advising the building contract. They become furious when the subject is mentioned.

Meanwhile, Lieutenant Hersing has sunk two English battleships near the Dardanelles with his *U-21* and has forced the English to reboard their troops again and to give up the project there. Everyone is talking about the German U-boat commanders.

Their Austrian comrades are enthusiastic about their stories and rejoice at their successes, but humiliation eats away at their hearts. Scarcely anyone speaks of it. They could accomplish the same, if only they had the boats for it. They are surely, always, "only the poor Austrians!"

Nine. *Giuseppe Garibaldi*

The expected answer to the bombardment of the Italian coast comes in slowly.

The Italians establish themselves on Pelagosa, a small, rocky island in the middle of the Adriatic. A lighthouse, visible from far away, stands on the highest point of the island; there the lighthouse keepers' families live. They are the island's only inhabitants.

From this island the Italians inch their way. They fire on the lighthouses of the islands spread out in front of Pelagosa and cut the telegraph cable.

Then they come nearer still.

One morning the signal station Klinči reports the approach of a flotilla on a course set toward Ragusa.[1] U-4 lies damaged with dismantled engines in the Gulf of Cattaro. Hurriedly, her crew assembles everything and the boat goes out half-ready to cut off the enemy.

In the meantime, an Italian cruiser and some destroyers try to destroy the signal station on the island of Giuppana and to cut the cable, but are averted by the cable guard.

Meantime, the main striking force, the armored cruiser division of the *Garibaldi* class, has approached Gravosa and shelled the harbor installations and the railway. Near Ragusa is the only point where the tracks can be seen from the sea. The Italian shells are intended to destroy the train lines and thus sever the connection between the Bocche and the interior. Meanwhile, Lieutenant Singule hurries toward Ragusa with his U-4. En route his men try frantically to make the boat submersible, and with great ingenuity and the help of many hands, the underwater journey is managed just as the enemy comes in sight.

The U-boat arrives exactly at the right moment, right in the middle of the shelling. It singles out the flagship, the *Giuseppe Garibaldi*, and sinks her with two torpedoes.

The remaining ships scatter, the destroyers hoist the Geneva flag with the red cross and rescue the survivors of their flagship. Meanwhile, they fire at the periscope of the submarine; Singule wonders about that, considering the flags that they are now flying! But he lets them finish their rescue operations.

He is completely unaware that with his direct hit he has saved the homeland's coast from further bombardments, and for the remainder of the war, the enemy, so superior in numbers, feels no urge to press on into the northern Adriatic.

Ten. *Nereide*

U-5 is moored in a small harbor at Lissa alongside Comisa's breakwater.

The pilots have reported an enemy U-boat lying at Pelagosa for defense of the island. The flotillas were fired at several times during the last shelling and now *U-5* is to bring down her Italian counterpart.

The sun bakes the deck. There is no breeze stirring in the harbor and the iron plates of the boat are so hot that the men put on their shoes. In the boat alone the thermometer reads 60 degrees Celsius.[1] In the shade of the dock there are blankets under which the crew and we two officers seek refuge from the burning sun.

The mayor has come to greet us. He is still angered about the latest visit of the French destroyers. Over in San Giorgio, on the other side of the island, they had exacted a "war contribution" and taken him captive. With greatest pains the small town had raised barely a portion of the demanded ransom money when the smokestacks of the Austro-Hungarian fleet came in sight.

"They dropped everything and made off, like young rascals who have rung the bell of a house door when the owner comes! Damn, it is a pity they already had the money!"

In the evening a fresh northeast wind springs up and *U-5* puts out to sea to creep up on Pelagosa in the darkness.

At sea, we encounter a storm.

Like horizontal rain the wind carries the spray before it, and wraps everything in white foam. The heavy seas make our small U-boat roll and it looks as if it were wallowing slowly before the wind through waves and troughs.

It is a terrific scene: these oncoming high waves, their crests breaking in the wind in their eagerness to go faster. Their dazzling white spumes give the most wonderful contrast to the deep blue of the water. Always there are three powerful waves, one after the other, and then it is as if there were a rest to collect power for the next thrust, until a water mountain once again

Fig. 9. On the residence ship *Crown Prince Rudolf*

raises itself high to try to bury the small boat. But, small as she is, she will not be destroyed. Like a boulder in the surf, she always stands there again, warding off every pounding, defying the brutal force of nature. Only sometimes, when a breaker is particularly heavy, a trembling goes through the boat's hull, as if the whole boat wanted to shake itself angrily, "Stop your silly jokes!" and like an answer the next wave comes soon and grabs those on watch on the tower up to their hips.

Those of us on watch care little for the sea's sense of humor. We have fastened ourselves to the small tower's handrail to prevent being washed away. As much as possible, we have dressed in watertight gear: boots and tar-impregnated clothes, with sleeves and trouser legs tied off with cord, and a hand towel stuffed around the throat that can be wrung out in calm moments to provide further service as caulking.

The tower hatches cannot be completely closed because the slow-running engines need to get air. Through the narrow opening one torrent after another pours into the boat, to the

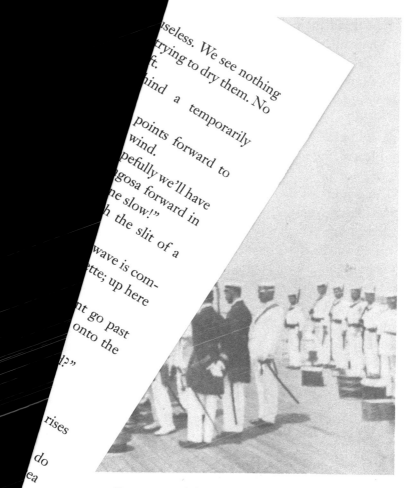

seless. We see nothing
rying to dry them. No
ft.
ind a temporarily
points forward to
wind.
pefully we'll have
gosa forward in
ne slow!"
h the slit of a

wave is com-
tte; up here

nt go past
onto the

l?"

rises

do
ea

ıg. 10. Decoration of the crew of S.M.U. 5 on the
flagship of the 5th Ship's Division

.cement of the cozy atmosphere below. The lookout looks
.ly ahead; he has to watch the forward horizon. The petty
.ficer on watch stands with his back toward the bow and looks
aft. The watch officer observes the water on all sides.

It is an arduous lookout. A periscope cannot generally be
seen in the spraying sea, and in this weather the boat could not
elude a torpedo. Today its wake would hardly be seen. The night

binoculars hanging from our necks are
through the wet lenses and have given up
one has even a half usable handkerchief le

Communication is only possible be
stretched sail canvas.

"Land ahead!" yells the lookout, and he
make himself understood despite the howling

Pleased, the watch officer nods his head: "Ho
luck once again! But go below and report: Pel
view, sunset, weather unchanged, starboard eng

"Hello Seyffertitz," I call from below throug
hatch, "Can I come up?"

The watch officer bends down: "One moment, a
ing right now. But I would be grateful for a lit cigar
we are out of dry matches!"

I step aside, light two cigarettes, and let the torre
him. Then I lift the hatch cover and force myself up
conning tower.

"Well, is everybody still here? No one gone overboar

"Sir, forward . . ."

"Thank you, I can see!"

Against the red evening sky the ridge of the rocky island
sharply.

"By the way, I am pleased that we have such weather. We
not know where this Italian U-boat lies. At any event, in this s
she has taken refuge on the lee side!"

"Sir, the wind seems to be dropping; the night will be qui
eter."

"You could be right. When the sea has calmed down a bit, we
will stop; otherwise we will drift too far down the coast.

"Now we still have 12 miles to Pelagosa. I suspect the Ital-
ians are in the large bay on the south side. Before dawn, around
3:30, we will dive before we get to the bay; then we will have
to look to see if we find anything. In any case, we must not be
seen; therefore, we will stay 3 miles from land. Don't let anyone

dare to light a cigarette up here. If they have even a half-good lookout, he would see the cigarette glow. By the way, what are we getting for supper?"

"Oh, today we can celebrate! This morning in Comisa we received some gifts of provisions. The mayor himself was there and brought a pile of fruit and fresh fish for everyone, and the bread was still warm."

"Terrific, aren't they nice people! But give the cook a man to help him hold the pans, otherwise he will spill all the good stuff. And then hit the sack for a while!"

"Have a good watch!" and the watch officer goes below.

Below everything is in one room, an entanglement of pipes, valves, levers, and engines. It seems disorganized, yet everyone knows what each thing is used for.

In the narrow passage between the engines the petty officers stand in uncomfortable positions, checking out the bearings and constantly wiping sweat from their foreheads with oakum that apparently never leaves their hands.[2]

Everything is damp. Water drips incessantly from the ceiling overhead, which is finished off with small cork pieces.

Those off duty lie on woolen blankets on the deck. There are no berths. They cover their faces because of the water drips.

The cook has jammed himself between his small electric cooking stove and a cupboard. He juggles his pans from which promising aromas of fried fish and hot oil are streaming.

The relieved watch rip the wet clothes from their bodies; the meal is still a quarter of an hour away. They can still sleep a bit.

Beside the torpedo tube two air mattresses lie on the deck. They are the berths for the two officers; they date from 1908 and are not airtight anymore. It makes no sense to try to keep them inflated because the air inside does not last very long. Seyffertitz lies down by the mattress and begins to inflate it; thirty-five breaths is the tested amount. Then the air lasts until you are asleep, provided that you can do it quickly.

During the night the U-boat reaches the proposed place.

There is plenty of time to dive; everything can be prepared calmly. First we ventilate the boat to rid her of gasoline and exhaust fumes.

During the night the wind drops, and the boat lies calm in the shelter of the island. Except for two men the whole crew is on deck. A few of them rub the sleep out of their eyes and pump their lungs with fresh air. Whoever still has tobacco rolls himself a cigarette, reaches down in the boat for it to be lit, and then he smokes it hidden in the hollow of his hand.

Suddenly the boat lights up in a bright glow.

"Telephone buoy disconnected!" shouts a voice from the tower into the boat.[3]

"For Pete's sake, who turned on the light? If the Italians are not sleeping like marmots, our trip has been in vain."

"Seyffertitz, when we get home, throw the whole thing out; we don't really need it. If we ever go belly up, no one will want to telephone us anyway. This is war!"

"Yes, sir . . . Telephone buoy to be dismantled and unloaded," reiterates the second officer in his best German.

By now dawn is slowly breaking and the boat must go underwater before she is detected.

At first she travels at fair speed. So far from land the streaks of foam from the periscope wake are hidden by whitecaps. I stand at the periscope. The crew's eyes fix tensely on my expression; only occasionally can I give any clues as to what I see.

The island's silhouette becomes increasingly distinct. On the rocks above, the large lighthouse is entirely clear and now the rays of the rising sun light up the bare rocks of the steep coast. No green is visible; the whole thing is gray and black. Only inside the bay, on the one place where a flat beach rises, smooth white stones are visible in contrast to the dark, steep, jutting rocks.

No living creatures can be seen; except for the lighthouse, there are no buildings. Nothing indicates an Italian occupation of the island.

"Have the Italians already left? You can see absolutely nothing!" I mutter to myself. "Or are they all still asleep?"

"Starboard five!" This command is intended for the helm. "At this time, would she be stationed underwater in front of the island?" And again back to the helm, "Forward!"

The torpedoes are reported "ready."

The U-boat travels in the bay ever closer to the coast until she is 300 meters from the shore. Strained, I look through the periscope, meter by meter, inspecting the shore and rocks for the enemy. Sweat drips from my forehead and my shirt sticks like a wet rag to my back. From time to time I wipe the eyepiece, which constantly mists over and impedes the view.

"If they bring a U-boat in here there must be a dock or something like that visible. She cannot always ride at anchor . . . Now we have traveled the length and breadth of the whole bay. I can't see anything . . . Hammer, steer her 1 meter higher!"

The boat comes slowly higher and the thick part of the periscope, which carries the magnifying lens, slides out of the water, producing a wide wake. The periscope searches the coast thoroughly. There—

"Full starboard, depth 12 meters, both torpedoes ready! How is our course?"

I have no time for explanations. With the magnification of the periscope, I have discovered the green, white, and red flag Barely above the shore the contrasting colors are visible against the dark rocks. Now I also see the U-boat itself, close to the land. With her gray color she is hardly visible. The boat's crew is washing on the beach. Then some of them point toward us; a couple of the men are already running to their boat.

"Course 140 degrees, torpedoes are ready, depth 12 meters," the answers are handed in one after the other.

Who is the faster now—and the calmer?

I had discovered the enemy too late and had already gone by her. It is no longer feasible to turn toward her directly. The U-boats are too close to each other. I must aim with the whole U-boat in order to fire the torpedo. Thus I must circle to starboard and get the enemy in front of the bow. But until then she must not see me. She must not know what I intend to do!

These thoughts go through my head. I step to the compass. The periscope is completely underwater and I would see nothing but the green of the water. On the compass-rose I see how the boat is turning: 180 degrees—225—270—320!

"Steer up for a lookout." The boat comes slowly higher.

"Shift rudder," the rudder should stop the momentum to starboard.

I look through the periscope again. What has the enemy possibly done in the meantime?

Now for a quick look. The eyepiece begins to break through the water's swell. How long it's taking today! Finally the sight is free.

"Completely to port!"

The Italian U-boat had already cast off from land, pointed her starboard side toward us, and is already half-submerged. One man still stands on the conning tower and appears to be calling something down into the boat.

This type of Italian boat can torpedo at 35 degrees from her course and has us right in front of her torpedo tubes. I have swung too wide, overshot the course toward my adversary, and must now turn back in order to be able to shoot.

The Italian has the advantage.

Will the U-boat never turn?

"Are you completely to port?"

"Rudder is completely to port!"

There . . . at first a few bubbles, which ascend in front of the Italian. They form a streak that runs uncannily quickly toward us.

The crash and end must be coming at any moment.

Or can we still pass?

"Propeller starboard!" call a couple of men. We distinctly hear the churning of the enemy torpedo as it streaks by through the water.

So—but now it's our turn!

The periscope line of sight shifts noticeably. Whether and how fast the enemy is traveling is not to be gauged in a rush. So, one torpedo in front of the bow, the other in the middle of the conning tower.

"Starboard torpedo—released!"

"Port torpedo—released!"

All nerves are tense to breaking. I chew on my moustache while I follow the path of the torpedoes. I can feel all eyes fixed on me.

The first torpedo overshoots the bow; the other has good aim.

"If only she doesn't go too deep, the distance is only 150 meters!"

Now—a tall burst of water and a dark cloud of smoke after, simultaneous with a shock that shakes our whole boat.

The water patters down again; the smoke goes away. Nothing is visible.

"Poor devil," escapes from my lips, but immediately after: "Left engine in reverse!" I must turn fast in order to get free from land.

Another look through the periscope.

A navy man with his hands on his back, in white trousers and a blue trimmed uniform walks on the peaceful shore.

Does he belong to the boat and did he come too late? If so, he can be glad about it.

U-5 has turned away and steered toward the sea.

By then everything on the island has become full of life. People stand together on the ridge; a few run down the slope. Then lightning flashes on top and white smoke clouds indicate that guns have gone into action. Bullets spray around the boat.

"Hammer," I call to the torpedo master. "Go 20 meters deep; the whole boat is exposed!"

In the shallow water the abnormally strong shock of the explosion had bent the indicator of the depth-pressure gauge, so the boat had come out of its dive.

"It really isn't necessary to let ourselves be shot at, at this point." I turn from the periscope and look around our boat.

The men stand silently at their stations. Their eyes show neither triumph nor victory. Only release from the tension. At best the feeling of satisfaction that once again they have performed their jobs well.

What happened above they could only surmise. They heard orders and followed them, they heard the torpedo rush by and tried, by reading my expression, to see whether it was serious, and trusted I would "do it."

I nod to them with appreciation and joy.

One man steps up to me: "I congratulate you, Sir!" and hands me a tumbler of champagne.

"Cheers, men!" Obediently I drink down the warm stuff.

"Thank you, Hermann! Where did you get this?"

"It is the last bottle from our packages from home; we kept it to celebrate the next direct hit!"

While the boat continues its quiet, unseen run underwater, I recount what just happened. Strange—my words come slowly. I had handled the situation more or less intuitively. There had not been enough time for deliberation—but now I should confirm my actions. I take out matches and illustrate the maneuver.

The whole thing had been so easy and so obvious!

"But I don't understand the Italians! No nets around the U-boat—no mines! Or did we only slide by? And why did she raise her flag at 5:00 in the morning? Without the bright colors I never would have discovered the boat!

"But now we will surface; we are out of their cannon's range."

The boat surfaces. One gas engine is turned on, and through the open hatch cover, a stream of fresh air surges into the steamy hot atmosphere of the boat. A light southwest breeze has set in and the moving air pleasantly dries up the perspiration-soaked bodies.

First a cigarette. Smoking is not allowed below. Besides, no matches will burn after an hour in the closed-up U-boat.

"Those guys must feel cheated," says one of the men and points with his thumb toward the ever-diminishing land. "First we sink their U-boat in front of their noses; now they see us leaving and can't do anything about it."

"If we were to leeward, we could hear them gnashing their teeth," laughs another in the stern. "And where do we go now?"

"The captain said something about Brindisi, but what will we find over there? At best one torpedo boat."

The engine runs irregularly and then stands still. She starts again, makes a couple of revolutions, and stops once more.

"What's wrong? What's the matter?" A call to those below.

A perspiration-soaked face appears suddenly in the hatch opening.

"Sir, I am sorry to report that gasoline cannot get through to the engine. The pipeline is blocked. Can I continue with the other engine?"

"Yes."

The gasoline pipelines are examined. The filters are full of flakes of varnish that have peeled off in the gas tank from the force of the explosion; now they are stopping up the pipelines.

The other engine runs for a while, then it also fails. After half an hour the first one works again.

"If this continues, we will have to pull in! In this situation we cannot charge the batteries," I call over to the second in command.

"Now both engines are broken!"

Both engines have stopped and the exhausted face of the engine master appears in the hatch. "Sir, it isn't working. I must clean all the pipelines."

Immediately I set to work with my men. We dismantle and clean the pipeline.

Seawater has leaked into the freshwater tank. The tank has sprung a leak from the force of the explosion.

So there is no more drinking water.

The men collapse on the engine from the gas fumes. The whole boat reeks of gasoline. The boat is ventilated and the men are brought on deck.

As soon as they barely recover, the work goes on.

Finally the pipelines are clear once again and the engines run.

But after one minute the engines stop. The whole gas tank must be full of varnish flakes.

"Grün, ignore this and send your men on deck. Travel electrically from now on!" I turn to my second officer, "We are going home; set the course toward the Bocche!"

It doesn't take long, then a coupling joint runs hot and only one motor can be kept in operation. So the morning of the next day U-5 limps into her harbor. On the same day the fleet commander flashes to the whole world: "On the fifth of this month at 5:00 in the morning our U-5 sank the Italian submarine *Nereide* at Pelagosa."

The response comes from across the sea: "Barbarians, pigs!"

Eleven. The Prize

Since the Italian declaration of war, the freighters of the Puglia line, which had supplied Montenegro, have stayed away. Instead, Greek and other neutral cargo vessels travel with weapons and ammunition, clothes, coal, and food to Montenegro. But all these goods have been declared by Austria as "contraband," and the U-boats have instructions to capture freighters that bring such banned goods to Montenegro. When that is not possible, they should sink the ships.

In the Drin Gulf we encounter sailing vessels and, from time to time, steamers, but they are all headed to San Giovanni di Medua, in neutral Albania, and we must let them go. At best, we can learn from them where they came across enemy warships in the Mediterranean.

The information is always the same: the blockade line has drawn back to the latitude of Cape Spartivento—the toe of Italy.

"It seems to me the *Léon Gambetta* has had an effect!" Seyffertitz tells me when he hears this news.

U-5 travels around to the Albanian coast and looks for a large steamer that, it had been reported, was proceeding toward Montenegro. It should be a big, wide one, approximately 20,000 tons.

But no matter how hard we look, she does not appear. Instead, one morning a smaller cargo vessel comes in sight in front of Durazzo. She is lit up as if in peacetime. Probably a neutral boat.

It is still too dark to know how to judge her; *U-5* alters her course and stays ahead of her in order to wait for the upcoming daylight.

Then she submerges.

"I see no guns, so we could surface again," I say at the periscope to my second in command. "But first get the artillery ready!"

The "artillery" is a small type 37-mm gun. It is not very formidable, designed more for sound effect.

The gunner shoulders it and waits for the boat to surface in order to install his gun on its pivot.

According to regulations, the first shot is fired across the bow to request the captain to stop.

But he continues on serenely.

"Either they didn't see us or they don't want to see us!" says the watch officer, and then above to the gunner: "Shoot above him!"

This works. The engines reverse and the cargo vessel comes to a standstill.

With the megaphone, the large mouthpiece, the captain is hailed; he is told to come on board *U-5* with his papers.

But the captain doesn't understand. At least he doesn't understand German. Then I try Italian, then English, French, even Croatian, when all else fails. Meanwhile, over there the Greek flag goes up.

"Does anyone know Greek?"

This is a most unusual situation—that, on an Austro-Hungarian warship there should be a dilemma due to language. But really no one speaks Greek. Also, you cannot speak well with hand signals at a distance. The gunner has a good idea: he aims with his gun at the bridge of the vessel.

All of a sudden the Greek understands.

"*Vengo . . . vengooo . . .*" resounds from over there, the rest is unintelligible but it sounds reassuring and confirming.[1] The men on the steamer run to lower a boat. Shortly the captain is rowed over, and he brings his identification papers with him. But these are not much help because they are drawn up in Greek. However, the captain suddenly speaks quite good Italian: "Steamer *Cephalonia* with 2,000 tons coal, corn, paper, and imitation leather cleared directly to Montenegro."

They have not yet discovered the trick of the detour via Albania! So, finally a good catch!

The captain is very upset. What bad luck! Until recently Italian torpedo boats had escorted him; they left him just half an hour before and assured him that nothing more could happen to him, and that the Austrians were afraid anyway! At that a couple of swear words slip out of him.

Well, nothing is to be done about it now.

When he returns to his ship, he is no longer the commander. Instead, the officer who came over with four men from the U-boat takes command.

Captor and captive travel side by side toward the Gulf of Cattaro.

It is always possible that enemy vessels show up, so I make

hand signals to the other boat: "All boats lowered to waterline. Everyone ready to abandon ship! If the enemy comes in sight, this vessel will be sunk."

The tranquility aboard the vessel is visibly disturbed. The life boats, which for years had been hanging from their davits, appear hydrophobic, because it takes a long time before they are packed full with boxes and sacks and hang on the ship's sides. But, undisturbed, U-boat and cargo vessel succeed in reaching the minefield in front of the Gulf of Cattaro.

So that the freighter's crew would not be able to locate the minefield, they are locked down below. The captain, who doesn't know what that means, becomes afraid and screams, "He's murdering us! He's murdering us!"

But he is reassured.

A destroyer takes over and tows the freighter into the harbor.

Everything had gone beautifully and bloodlessly—but at the last moment there is a casualty. One of the men manages to shoot himself in the foot when unloading his pistol!

The only injury of the whole war on my boats.

Twelve. Gasoline Stupor

The lighthouse on Lagosta reports: "Twenty nautical miles out to sea toward Lagosta a light cruiser *Quarto* type sighted."

The same day *U-5* leaves Rose. The Italians could have designs on the islands that extend up and down the Dalmatian coast and return!

That evening the boat waits 20 nautical miles southeast of Lagosta.

The night is misty; a severe thunderstorm approaches and bolts of lightning flash into the water one after another, blinding the eyes. The downpour destroys all visibility and it is pointless to stay above water. An attack is out of the question; at worst we might be rammed unexpectedly. For that reason, I decide to spend the night underwater. At the same time, that will spare the

Fig. 11. S.M.U. 5 at the dock in Comisa

crew. Two at both rudders, two others for the electric motors and the bilge pump. All the others can sleep.

It is very cozy on board. We are 25 meters below the surface, at the slowest speed that keeps the boat maneuverable. Everything is quiet, and only now and then the high pitch of the bilge pump interrupts the stillness. The pump must constantly empty the bilge, where incoming water collects through small, porous leaks.

The underwater rest is especially beneficial to the mechanics, since they seldom rest. They can barely sleep their fill when the boat is in her harbor because there is so much work to do on the ancient engine.

We two officers relieve each other, checking the depth as well as the course and letting the bilge pump work when the boat becomes too heavy. She should travel underwater at bare steerage, the diving rudder keeping her at the ordered depth.

At dawn the boat resurfaces again.

Everyone's lungs need fresh air after the stifling atmosphere that developed overnight in the boat.

Fig. 12. The Italian U-boat *Nereide*

The thunderstorm has blown over, wind and sea have sub-
sided, and the boat lies stopped while the engines charge the
batteries and fill the air cylinders.

A dark, thick bank of fog lies toward Italy; it slowly rolls toward the boat. It stands there like a wall, sharply contrasting
with the blue of the sea. It is approximately only six miles away;
therefore, we must keep watch in this direction.

The men have made themselves comfortable on deck and
smoke their long-awaited cigarettes. Some of them swim alongside the boat. Only those on watch are on the lookout.

Suddenly the cry: "Shut off the engines—emergency dive—
turn on the ventilators!"

Like ripe plums the men drop into the boat through the tower.
The deck is already awash as the last swimmer reaches the railing and dashes up and over to the conning tower. The hatch is
barely closed as the sea rushes over the sinking boat. This all
has happened so fast that the dive can be stopped only at 30 meters—and only then the boat is raised to periscope level.

"What's happened? Did you see something?"

"Didn't you see her? An Italian cruiser—*Quarto* type. All at
once she was there in full view. She came through the fog as if
it were a curtain. It's a miracle they didn't see us. Not six miles
away! She is coming directly toward us."

"Both torpedoes ready, both engines slowly forward!"

I watch the Italian boat through the periscope, and as I glance up, one of the crewmen is brought forward and laid on the floor.

"What does he have?"

"Gasoline stupor, sir!"

"So soon—What else can we expect?"

The opponent had come into view so suddenly that, in the hurry to go underwater unseen, we couldn't think of ventilating the boat.

A couple of minutes later, five men lie poisoned and unconscious on the floor, and the rest who are still able to work are overcome by a nausea and a headache that feels as if an iron hoop were clamped around their head. In addition, we feel extremely drowsy and must fight that with all our willpower.

Two more men collapse and only three men and we two officers are left to operate the entire boat.

At the moment of the attack, the torpedo master mans the diving rudder, one man is at the helm, the second officer clears the torpedoes, and the machinist mate operates the engines and helps me turn the periscope.

The cruiser moves slowly, much too slowly for me, as I have to fire before the other four and I collapse. After each lookout I correct my course and speed. The closer we two enemies get, the slower our U-boat has to travel so that the periscope doesn't create a wake.

Suddenly I feel as if the floor were giving way under my feet; I have to sit down on a folding stool in front of the periscope.

"Hermann, wake me in three minutes! Ten degrees starboard!" And I collapse on my seat.

The machinist mate stands with his watch in his hand and shakes me awake.

The boat again steers for a lookout.

"Wake me in one minute!" Then: "Wake me in thirty seconds!"

"In ten seconds!"

Now the boat can maneuver into firing position.

"Sixty degrees to port, both torpedoes ready to fire!"

"They are ready," the answer comes.

Just don't give in now—just hang in there for a few more minutes; any moment now!"

"Hammer should go on the lookout."

"Sir, the boat is too heavy in the bow, I can't manage the weight in the bow with the helm!"

"Both engines full speed!"

With increased speed the man at the diving rudder succeeds in bringing the boat on an even keel and then he steers the boat upward in order to get the periscope out of the water. At that we hear a rushing sound in the bilge and the water that has collected runs aft. With the last few men who were staying upright with their last ounce of strength, it was impossible to operate the bilge pumps as well.

Three, four minutes have passed since the last sighting of the enemy and I should have checked the cruiser long ago. Where did she go in the meantime? It's a matter of seconds! In never-ending intervals the report comes from the diving rudder: "15 meters . . . 14 meters . . . 12 meters . . . 10 meters . . ."

At that the periscope breaks through the surface.

I can see nothing.

I turn the periscope in all directions. Aft I see only water, forward the sky. The boat has emerged so steeply with her heavily laden stern that the periscope radius goes beyond the cruiser.

U-5 shoots nearly completely out of the water, the bow smacks downward again, and finally the cruiser can be seen in the periscope. The enemy ship has already gone past our course; coming about is not possible because the cruiser has turned. The enemy ship steers at full speed toward the wake of U-5 where she is in no danger.

Through the periscope you can see the gunners running to their guns; then our boat submerges again, and at the next lookout the cruiser is already far away.

After a quarter of an hour U-5 surfaces.

The cruiser is still well in sight, but she does not know the circumstances on the U-boat. Otherwise she would return quietly and harvest a cheap victory. Underwater, with no one at the controls, the boat would have slowly settled to the bottom, and on the surface the enemy would have had the easy target of a defenseless opponent.

After U-5 has been ventilated, a couple of men come to, the others are brought with difficulty up the steep iron ladder through the narrow conning tower on deck, and the semiconscious must resuscitate their remaining comrades and bring them back to life.

"Such a pity," I comment, "such an opportunity will not come again. She would have been ours for sure."

"And with such junk we must wage a war!"

Thirteen. America Bluffs

In the summer of 1916 many German U-boats come to the Adriatic. The place is crawling with them, both in the Bocche and in Pola, where they are overhauled when they return from their long trips in the Mediterranean.

There is still more work for them to do here, whereas in the North Sea and around England, the steamship war is slowly being snuffed out. It is essentially the fear of a declaration of war by the United States that causes Bethmann-Hollweg, the German Chancellor, to impose new restrictions on U-boats in their war on trade ships. In effect, he wrenches the currently most effective weapon out of Germany's hand.

President Wilson has openly joined England's side. He wants to eliminate the Central Powers' most dangerous weapon, the U-boats, and with the cheap slogan: "upholding the most sacred of human rights" he pushes for the safe passage of passenger steamers. A free American citizen must be able to move about wherever he wants to, and on every steamer—even English ones—he must be certain of his life.

At the same time, those transports filled with munitions and troops are dispatched to England and are armed.

So woe if a Yankee war supplier gets a scratch when he happens to go to England to conclude his business!

It is only luck that they have no business transactions in enemy trenches; if they had, they might also have to be under protection there.

All the neutral countries supply England. They, too, want to get free passage. A flood of regulations pours over the U-boats. Today they are still allowed to sink this and that type of steamer; tomorrow they may not. No one knows what is going on any more.

Finally the war on commercial ships dies, although the German naval command pushes to gain unlimited U-boat war.

But Bethmann-Hollweg is upheld and has his way. The American bluff worked.

The war on commercial ships can continue only in the Mediterranean. No Americans seem to be sailing here.

Fourteen. The First Depth Charges

"*U-4* is arriving," the signalman of the *Dalmat* advises in the officers' mess.

"Hello, Singule, what's up?"

"We torpedoed an English cruiser, *Weymouth* type; she did not sink. They have invented something new!"

Later, in the officers' mess he recounts: "I am lying near Cape Pali and then a *Weymouth* class ship comes toward me out of the Drin Gulf. She has five destroyers by her, protecting her in front and at the sides. I go to attack, dive under one destroyer and fire two shots. One torpedo misses, the other hits an engine room.

"Then the destroyers come on, firing away, and I dive to 20 meters. But the firing doesn't stop. That is to say, we hear continuous explosions. I cannot understand it; they could not see me so the shooting seems pointless. After a while I look and see explosions in the water here and there around the destroyers. They must have some kind of bombs that explode underwater.

"They are not powerful; I think the English only want to scare us and still we could hear the explosions from far away!"

"Indeed, that is something new. But you will see, once they make more powerful bombs, we will have to watch out. With these they could spring a leak in our fuel tanks. Especially your Germania boats with your thin outboard tanks."

"They seem to think up new deviltries," says another. "The other day the German *U-10* sighted a U-boat off the coast of Venice. As he approached to attack, this thing seemed so strange. It lurched so peculiarly in the lifeless sea! As he came closer, he saw that the U-boat lay at anchor on a monster of a chain that no U-boat could have. He looked at it and saw that the chaps had put the superstructure of a U-boat on a raft to simulate a U-boat. Probably there were mines placed all around. Once he saw that, he left immediately.

"The other day a pilot told me this story. He had been sent to Brindisi to drop his bombs over there. Naturally they shot at him and, for some reason, he flew very low. There he saw a stick in the water and thought it was a periscope, but he had no more bombs. He wanted to at least get a look at the supposed U-boat. As he flew over it, he discovered a mine on which the 'periscope,' an ordinary stick, was attached. Undoubtedly, one of our torpedo boats was meant to have rammed it!"

"Nowadays we have to be careful, or the war might get dangerous!"

"Look here, how sharp-witted you can be!"

"Cheers, Singule, to the next one."

Fifteen. **Heroes**

"*U-3* is overdue. She should have arrived long ago."

We officers of the U-boat station sit together in the officers' mess of the *Dalmat*, a small navy yacht that was assigned to us as our residence ship.

"Also Lerch has not returned; today the news came from Italy that one of our U-boats hit mines outside Venice. That can only be *U-12*."

We sit silently at our table. Lerch, one of our best and most beloved comrades! Always cheerful, full of fun, ready for anything. As we say in the navy, "a real shipmate" who would stop at nothing, whether he was out in search of adventure or going out against the enemy. About whom the funniest stories were told. Every boat commander literally tore himself apart to get him because he was so competent.

One lifts his glass: "To our Lerch, his second, Zecharaiah, and his men . . ."

"God willing, Strnad will come back!"

"And if not, who will be the third?"

We look at one another. The triplicate of tragedies had already become proverbial in the war.

"Wasn't Lerch your second for a long time?" someone asks me.

"Yes, on *U-6*. Still before the war. I liked him very much . . . He tore himself apart for me . . . A great friend."

I get up and go on deck. I cannot stand it below any longer. My last conversation with Lerch comes back to me. Lerch had grumbled: "They don't let me in the Bocche; I have to stay in Pola. But there is nothing to catch. My boat belongs at sea!' and then he asked me: "What would you do in my place?"

"Well, Lerch," I had answered then, "If we do not know where to find something better in the Bocche, we go to Brindisi. Perhaps you could find something outside Venice. There is still a chance . . . possibly you could explore the entrance through the mines. Supposedly ships ride at anchor there. But be careful!"

"You're right. I'll just take a look around there . . ." were his last words.

Now this conversation goes through my head. I feel remorseful. I gave my friend advice that perhaps brought him and his boat to their deaths.

But it is always possible that this news is not true, as so many reports have already been.

He is overdue. Lerch is stubborn, and if he did not get to fight, he would stay out longer. Perhaps he would come back after all!

But after a couple of days the official message arrives: an Italian gunboat sighted the periscope of *U-12* and escaped into the minefield. Lerch had gone after him thinking that the enemy would follow the clear passage to Venice and, in so doing, ran into a mine. Apparently he didn't even consider that the gunboat, with its low draught, could go right over the mines.

Day after day passed and Strnad did not return with *U-3*. Only after a long time the news arrived that gave a rough description of his end: After lying unsuccessfully in ambush outside Brindisi, *U-3* fired a torpedo at the Italian auxiliary cruiser *Città di Catania*. The steamer evaded the torpedo and tried to ram the U-boat, grazed her, and dropped depth charges. Right after that an Italian torpedo boat approached the U-boat at full speed and launched two torpedoes that went above her. After that followed depth charges that made the periscope useless and punched leaks in the mufflers and some of the tanks. Then the torpedo boat lost the U-boat's wake because it had gone underwater badly damaged and tried to escape. In the afternoon *U-3* surfaced but had to go underwater immediately because a French cruiser was nearby. Finally at night she shook off her pursuers and could surface.

Then the men could see the extent of the damage. The engines did not work anymore. Every now and then they would start up, only to stop again. The men worked in despair to find the problem. Late that night, they found the cylinders were full of water. They continued the trip with the electric motors, and they tried to repair the damage at least temporarily. At that point three destroyers approached the boat. It was completely hopeless, but one last effort had to be made. The boat could hope to escape underwater, but the pumps no longer worked. During the dive, the incoming water ran forward, and with a bow weight of 40 degrees, the boat shot into the deep. More water constantly poured in from the increasing pressure; by this time the storage batteries were swamped, and the forming chlorine asphyxiated the men. Six men fell over one after the other. Then the electric motors broke down.

With that, the boat was finished.

Now all that mattered was to save the crew. They succeeded in blowing out the ballast tanks, and the boat shot from 30 meters' depth to the surface of the water. The last command rang out: "Every man abandon ship!"

Line officer Karl Strnad, the commander, stood in the tower. Everyone who left the ship to jump into the water had to pass him.

He stood smiling, leaning against the wall, shook each man's hand one last time and thanked him. Then he went below and sank with his boat into the deep.

An Austrian navy officer.

Two men were killed by gunfire from the destroyer; the rest were taken prisoner.

Sixteen. *Curie*

Until autumn 1915 the U-boat station in Rose expands. Five tiny U-boats, each dismantled in three parts, come by train from Germany. Each separate piece is ready to be assembled where it belongs. In Pola they are riveted together, pipelines and cables connected, and they are finished, ready to be used. No doubt these are small things with only one engine, but they are reliable. The boats have the most modern equipment and a large cruising radius. They can go underwater in twenty seconds.

But another, a sixth boat, is added as well.

In December 1914, the French U-boat *Curie* attempted to enter the port of Pola. She had been towed by a cruiser to the middle of the Adriatic and, near the entrance to the harbor at Pola, she managed to discover the mine passage by observing incoming ships; then she went as far as the long breakwater that was designed to protect the harbor from enemy U-boats.

A netting barricade was attached to the head of the long dock; this netting would be opened for arriving and departing ships. The heavy beams that carry this wire netting were drawn deep into the water by its weight so that they were hard to discover with a periscope.

The nets were the nemesis of the *Curie*. Free from the head of the breakwater, the U-boat steered toward the harbor and was caught. She tried to break loose and surfaced, but the netting went up with her and even her engines could not free her.

A shore battery lies facing the head of the dock. From there and from a vessel they noticed the barriers rocking, saw the surfacing tower, and riddled it with bullets. At that the boat sank, but surfaced immediately again with its entire body; the hatches on deck were pushed open and the crew jumped out and into the water. Then the boat sank. Her second officer was still standing in the tower; he had been hit in the chest.

In the meantime, the harbor was alerted and many boats rushed over to rescue the swimmers.

The *Curie* was then raised and restored; now she travels as *U-14* under the Austrian flag.

All countries keep the designs of their submarines confidential; thus there is a great stir as *U-14* takes her mooring in Rose.

She has a tiny tower, more like a higher hatch, behind which an iron scaffolding projects up with a platform, constituting the command post.

Three rudders serve for diving, which enable her also to make changes in depth and also in the horizontal position.

A torpedo shaft is forward in the bow's hold; six torpedoes

lie exposed outside on the boat's hull and can be launched from inside. Some can be fired forward, some broadside.

Inside there is a lot of room; bulkhead doors subdivide the boat so the engines and their noise can be cut off from the remaining space. The whole diving maneuver can be accomplished from one central control room where the helm and the gyrocompass are located. The periscope ends in this room as well.

The men have berths and there is even an officers' mess. Also, there are two watch officers on board, a great relief for the commander.

A short time after the arrival of *U-14*, her commander gets sick, and I take over the boat.

Once again it means parting from my old familiar crew who stood with me through all the hardships and dangers. It is also a difficult departure from the old boat herself. I know each of her sounds in my sleep, know how she reacts to all help, like a good horse; she has become a living thing for me, even if old and sick. My hand rests one more moment stroking the conning tower. Good old Number Five . . . then I shake myself and leave the boat.

Seventeen. The Oil Spill

I have gotten used to my new boat. I am not very delighted with it, although, in some respects, this boat has advantages over my old Number Five.

It worries me greatly that it is really an art to dive with this boat in heavy seas. In spite of everything, it sometimes takes a quarter of an hour to get underwater! This boat has outboard torpedoes. An accurate shot is not possible with them since the firing apparatus functions only with 10 degrees' precision. The mechanisms have not been worked through precisely. Everything is brilliantly thought out but not solidly constructed. Also, the engine is unreliable.

So I have exchanged old worries for new ones!

U-14 and *U-4* have thought out a joint venture. We want to be outside Durazzo in the morning and lie in ambush for arriving cargo steam ships. One of us would come from the south, one from the north.

At first we travel together into the Bay of Lales, which, protected against the south wind, lies directly north of Durazzo. You can also lie on the bottom when the weather is severe with siroccos so stormy that attacks are impossible. For this reason the Bay is most attractive and is nicknamed "Villa Lales." The bottom is muddy there and the boat lies smoothly as if in a bed.

U-14 is brought to a halt; after the report, "Everything watertight," the ballast tanks are flooded a couple of kilograms and the boat sinks slowly.

The hull has been tested to 2.5 atmospheric pressure; thus you can lie calmly at 25 meters' depth.

The depth gauge needle continues further: 10 meters, 15, 20, 21, 23 meters; then it stands still. It is barely noticeable that the boat touched down. Now more water is pumped into the tanks, to make the boat heavier and unable to be displaced by the current. Then it gets cozy.

The folding table in the officers' mess is set up. It lies directly in the passage from forward to aft, but at least, lying on the bottom, you can afford to lay a table. Whoever wants to go past must dive under it, but the men develop an incredible skill much like hurdlers.

The table is set with plates and glasses and you can eat like a civilized person. Even wine is poured for this special occasion and afterward cards are brought out because a game of Tarot can only add to the atmosphere.

The men celebrate also. The sound of an accordion comes from the bow and alternates with the gramophone that constantly plays, "O Blue Adriatic." A terrible song, but it appears to be either beloved, or one of the few records that is still whole.

Everyone can sleep tonight; only one watch stander watches over the depth gauge and the compass rose.

Morning brings us to the surface again. The tanks are emptied until the boat lifts itself from the bottom, but the mud will not let it go. The adhesion is too strong, and a lot of drive is required for it to break loose. Then the boat races up and the pumps empty the tanks completely.

"I beg to report the cocoa is ready."

Everything tastes of petroleum, the engine's fuel. Breakfast, the first cigarettes, even the pencil that a man who is working on the maps puts into his mouth. Even a kiss would taste like petroleum, but that has not been tested on board.

A couple of hundred meters' distance from our boat, U-4 surfaces. Our boats signal each other, "Have a good trip!" and each of us goes to his appointed post.

We see nothing the whole day. No ships and no planes.

While the engines run, they pump air into the partly used air tanks, and our boat scouts the route toward Brindisi.

At 9:00 in the evening the alarm sounds: "Emergency dive!"

In the dark, overcast night, a destroyer has suddenly appeared at a couple of hundred meters' distance.

Traveling at full speed, our boat turns away in order to show the enemy her narrow side.

"Every man forward!"

The bow sinks in the swell with the increased weight; the boat slants more forward, but does not submerge, as if the stern were being kept high.

"Are the air vents open?"

"They are open!"

"Everyone aft to level the keel!"

In one of the aft tanks, an air pocket must have formed that cannot escape. The boat rights herself again, finally the air whistles through the air vents, and then goes into the deep.

At the common deep sigh of relief, we notice how tense the last few minutes have been. We had expected the shock of being rammed at any moment but thank God—nothing moved.

"Vio, did you experience this before my time? You know the boat better than I," I ask my first officer.

"Sir, the air vents are too small and not situated at the highest point, so the air escapes only after a bit of rocking. We dove too suddenly with weight in the bow, so the air could not escape. We must have looked like a duck wagging its rump in the air."

"We will stay underwater for now."

At dawn the next morning the expected steamers come on their approach to Durazzo.

While the ships slowly become visible on the horizon and get bigger, I have time to position myself well. I want to launch my attack on a counter-course to the next steamer and to launch a torpedo broadside. I operate my periscope while balancing on a small, raised platform. I don't need to hide the periscope; there is not enough light yet. The attack is child's play. At 500 meters I am finally within range; I fire and watch the path of the torpedo.

"It's running completely crooked; it will never get there." The torpedo runs far aft, past the steamer.

"A fine job," I grumble. "It's a pity the engineer didn't ask my grandmother; then he would have produced something better than this piece of junk!"

Torpedo seven ready. At least the bow torpedo should run accurately.

But the second steamer is at too extreme an angle and a shot is impossible.

I rotate the periscope for a look all around.

There, a French torpedo boat is passing me at 50 meters' distance. A machine gun fiercely shoots at the periscope and the bullets splash all around the target. The sailor in his tasseled cap has an angry expression, as if to say, "Now I have you!"

I have to laugh.

"A Frenchman is shooting with his machine gun and the fool thinks he can do something to us," but then I think of the depth charges that must be imminent.

"Twenty meters' depth, both engines full force, full to port.

"Let's get out of here!"

But the boat has not yet been able to turn fully away, and when the first explosion comes, the boat is in darkness.

We can only feel her listing when the second depth charge comes, somewhat farther away but still strong enough to make the whole boat shudder.

No one knows what actually happened. At that point a man loses his nerve and screams: "Surface!"

No panic now.

"Quiet in the boat!"

The most important thing now is light. Portable accumulator batteries are at hand and with their help at least the course can be steered. Later we will find out if the fuses blew or the bulbs have been smashed.

One of the officers turns on the gramophone. How peculiar "O Blue Adriatic" sounds now, always interrupted by the crashes of the depth charges.

"Helm fails to work."

"Boat stuck at 15 meters," comes the report from the vertical and diving rudders.

The boat is lying on the bottom.

"Stop the engines!"

If possible, the mud should not be churned up, as it would betray the boat.

"Everyone listens for sounds: Grinding propellers come closer and move away again. Then bombs fall far away; finally it is quiet.

"Are we taking in water aft?"

"All secure aft."

"Are we taking in water forward?"

"All secure forward."

"Engine room, everything is watertight," the reports are submitted.

"Attention! We are stuck. Without blowing out the tanks, we

cannot get free with the engines alone. As soon as the boat is released from the bottom, both engines maximum force forward and immediately flood the tanks!

"Diving rudder, try to keep the boat under water, understood?"

"Yes, sir!"

The maneuver is executed just as had been explained. But the boat will not break away from the bottom and needs a lot of drive to separate. She cannot pick up forward speed quickly enough to prevent surfacing, and she breaks out of the water with her whole superstructure. With a quick look all around I see three destroyers rushing at me and firing, but my boat goes under again and steers at 14 meters' depth, toward deeper water.

"If they have a plane around, he would be able to see us—at 14 meters' depth."

Again we hear a depth charge exploding aft, but this time weaker and farther away.

"Now they are laying their eggs in our mud," says one, and he is not far wrong. The boat and the bombs must have turned up quite a mire.

With time *U-14* gains deep water and can continue at 20 meters.

The bilge pump is useless; its shaft has been broken by the explosions and the boat takes in abnormal amounts of water through leaks.

The next lookout finds the three destroyers aft of our boat; they are pursuing us at 1,500 meters in our wake.

The sea is as smooth as glass.

I veer 90 degrees and look out after a while. The destroyers are faithfully following me.

"They are still there. Could we be dragging anything?"

I search the wake thoroughly, but cannot see anything. Again I turn 90 degrees and go down to 20 meters.

"The destroyers must have sound detectors . . . How else can they track us?"

We stop every noise in the boat. The repair work that had begun at the pumps is discontinued. The helm is operated manually.

After half an hour at the next check, the pursuers are still there, only they have fallen farther behind. At 10 meters the trip goes on. The periscope is often used; the destroyers pick up speed and come closer.

Once more the U-boat turns 45 degrees and steers at 25 meters depth.

The bilge rises, the boat gets heavier, and the engines must run faster in order to maintain the depth.

"Sir, if we proceed very slowly, we have enough electric charge for two hours; then the battery will be drained," informs the electrician.

"That's good."

I fling myself on my berth.

The boat had gone twelve hours underwater now and the air contains only little oxygen. There is no equipment for reclaiming the air. Only the new boats have such things.

Now the situation becomes serious.

I know I must make a decision now; I breathe in short, hasty breaths. The heat in the boat is gruesome. The men at the helm pant from the work and continually wipe sweat from their eyes so they can see. Most of them have stripped almost to their skivvies; nevertheless, sweat drips off them in streams.

Whoever does not have to work is ordered to lie down in order to consume as little oxygen as possible.

Everyone has a heavy head. We breathe only intermittently with open mouths. The smallest motion becomes hard work . . . even concentrating.

I notice it all; I see the men repeatedly looking toward me, very quietly and so full of trust: "Have you thought of the solution yet?"

In the meantime, the pursuers won't be shaken off. Only a short while and the boat cannot stay underwater any longer. The doubling also has served no purpose.

Everyone waits for my decision.

Then I have it: the bombs must have punched leaks in the oil tanks and the destroyers are following the trail of the rising petroleum beads. On the glassy sea the iridescent colors must be quite distinct. And the deeper the boat goes, the longer the path of the discharged fuel to the surface, and the farther the destroyers fall behind.

That's it—everything makes sense to me.

I sit up. First I must get fresh air in here. I call both officers and the chief machinist and tell them my hypothesis.

"We will go now to 35 meters depth. The boat is tested only to 25, but she will stand it! Then the destroyers will drop back farther.

"You, Vio, steer up a bit as quickly as possible so I can see the situation. If the destroyers are far enough away, we will surface immediately.

"Meyerhofer, as soon as I open the hatch, you immediately put the engine into gear. That way air will be sucked into the boat. As soon as the command to dive comes, put it in neutral.

"Is that clear?"

The three go to their posts; then I hold back my youngest officer.

"Müller, now listen. When we surface, those fellows are going to shoot aft. They are not far away and their shots will fall very close to us. But they will not hit us because they will be coming too fast.

"Do you know how you can tell that a U-boat has been hit? By the famous oil spill. So we will create one for them!

"Get a bucket of oil and when the hatch is open, put it into my right hand."

The officer grins and nods.

Meanwhile, the boat has gone to 35 meters. It seems to creak . . . but that might be only my imagination.

"Vio, go ahead!"

The boat shoots upward. I stand at the periscope and look aft.

At 10 meters the boat is leveled off and the view is clear. The destroyers have stayed back at about 2,500 meters.

"Surface!"

The hatch is hardly free when I raise the lid and lean out.

"Hand me the bucket!"

In a large arc a flood of oil flies overboard. The destroyers have already accelerated. As if wearing white mustaches they come charging with their wakes boiling up, firing away so that the shots splash round about in the water.

"Ssss," some shells pass way above the boat. The engine has already pumped the boat full of fresh air and much of the stale air has been pushed outside through the exhaust.

"Emergency dive!"

The tower hatch is shut and immediately flooded.

Up to now everything has gone smoothly. Will the enemy be deceived?

With fresh air and the maneuver the men have become mobile again, and the cook is pressed for food. Soon full bowls are passed around.

There is something peculiar about the men in a U-boat. They are like one single organism, and the commander is simultaneously head and heart. Perhaps this exists nowhere else to such a degree. Wherever many men submit to one commander, whether in trenches, on a cruiser, a torpedo boat, an airplane . . . wherever else, each individual might not be able to talk with the commander; still he can look at him and think with him. Only in underwater journeys in U-boats, so to speak, eyes, ears, and thoughts for the individual are superfluous; the men are still only the hands and feet that carry out what their collective will, the commander, orders. But they are constantly aware that everything depends exactly on the precision and speed of their hands and feet as much as it depends on the brains that control all. By the same token, the hands and feet may be as clever and willing as can be, but they can accomplish nothing great if the head is weak or the heart is faint.

I know all this, too. I know my fear is theirs and my confidence is theirs. And because of that I must often somehow or other feign confidence with my last bit of energy when perhaps I really do not have any more left. Like now, for example. I may appear content as I look above the heads of my men as they eat. I consider: if I am not rid of the enemy, I must engage him in battle before the battery runs out. But I can no longer take him by surprise; that is impossible in view of the oil trail. In the mirrorlike water they would discover the periscope immediately.

And the navy possesses so few boats. She depends on each one.

I take my time before the next lookout.

Then I decide to look. Carefully I raise the periscope.

Aft nothing . . . then a quick look around . . . also nothing.

I can hardly believe it; I steer the boat higher, look once more, then surface and climb on deck. Far and wide no sign of the enemy. The entire horizon is clear.

Isn't it beautiful out in God's fresh air!

"They are gone," I call down below. "All tanks emptied, both engines on, and full speed ahead!"

The boat comes slowly higher out of the water like a whale. Officers and men hurry on deck and roll the unavoidable cigarettes.

During a cursory inspection of the boat, two fuel tanks are found to be leaking, all outboard torpedoes are crushed, and in their present condition unusable. Further damage can be ascertained at the dockyard.

In the Bocche both U-boats meet again.

U-4 had similar luck; by a hair's breadth she missed sinking an English cruiser.

On one of the following days the enemy reported the sinking of an Austrian U-boat at Durazzo. The decoration of the commander concerned is also mentioned.

We grant them this satisfaction.

Eighteen. Deck Paint

Along the northern coast of the island of Corfu *U-14* heads toward Santa Quaranta.

It has been eight years since I was in Corfu. The German Emperor had at that time undertaken a Mediterranean trip in his yacht, the *Hohenzollern*, and was staying in the Achilleion, the former property of Empress Elisabeth.[1] The officers of the squadron had been invited for an evening of beer drinking, during which we enjoyed ourselves and had a good time. Among other things on the program, His Majesty's entrances into German cities were shown on film.

The harbor at Corfu in neutral Greece is occupied by the French fleet, which had spun a web of mines and nets around itself. Signal stations are located on the island's mountains to report passing ships.

Once there, we remember that in her former life *U-14* was called *Curie* and was French; we immediately raise the French flag.

It was Vio's idea and with it he saved the boat another underwater trip. Everyone imagines himself secure under the protection of the Tricolor in enemy waters; even the old *Curie* seems comfortable flying her former colors.

It is after lunch and we three officers are standing on deck.

"What's wrong with the captain today?" asks Vio gently of the third. "Did something happen?"

"Nothing, surely it's the boat he is worried about," he murmurs back.

With a frown I had been inspecting my men who were lying around on deck looking obviously tired and sick. Now I turn to the other two with barely suppressed wrath.

"Just look at these men! The engine crew is completely exhausted. I believe it, too, when every two days they have to take apart one of the two engines. And they have hardly patched one

Fig. 13. A torpedo head crushed by depth charges

when the other breaks down. Besides, you never know if the boat will ever return home!"

"In her present condition, you cannot wage war with this boat," corroborates Vio emphatically. "It must be completely rebuilt. The engine is slowly falling apart and is, on the whole, a piece of junk."

Fig. 14. S.M.U. *14*, formerly *Curie*, during the overhaul in Pola

The jovial Müller grins surreptitiously. He knows that Vio enjoys nothing more than to discuss the present unsuitability of the boat. Day and night, he thinks about how and where you could improve her. For example, in order to speed up the diving process he has brought up the idea of an extra tank that would only be filled for the dive; once underwater, it would be emptied.

Then it starts to rain suggestions: improvements for the torpedo firing apparatus, a gun, a decent tower, and, naturally, new engines! It is like a wish list before Christmas. Now Müller and Vio summon the chief engineer; when he is first allowed to "wish" aloud, he can hardly stop. He and his engine crew are truly the first to suffer. They must constantly rebore the individual cylinders and copy their diagrams.[2] And these change constantly. The work never ceases, either at sea or in the harbor, and the men don't even know what a day of rest is.

Machinist mate Mayerhofer tells me: "The other day I asked one of the men, 'how long have you been on board?'

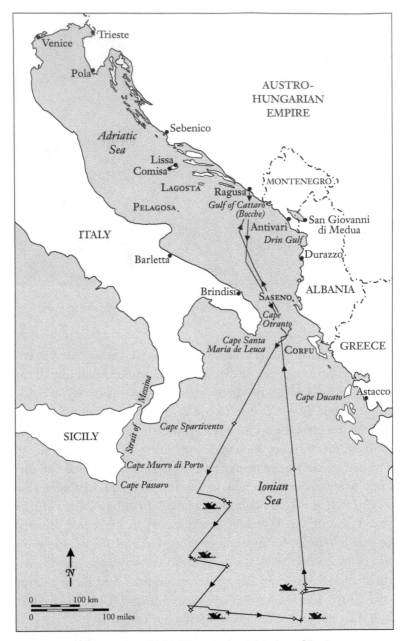

Fig. 15. The cruise of S.M.U. *14* in the Adriatic and Ionian seas,
August 20–September 1, 1917

"He looked up from his work and thought a moment: 'Not even a week.'

" 'Nonsense,' I said, 'you were brought on in Pola!'

" 'Yes, that's true,' he reckoned, 'but that was on a Sunday and since then I haven't had a second day off.'

"That was in May and now the summer is nearly over."

"Yes, something must happen, and soon, to be sure!" I reiterate, and we all become engrossed in the proposed reconstruction of the boat.

"Airplane!"

Somebody calls out. Everyone looks up.

"Where?"

"He's coming out of the sun!"

Gliding, completely silently, the airplane steers toward *U-14*. The distance decreases rapidly and the French colors shine obtrusively. You can see the bombs suspended and prepare to hear the imminent crash.

It would be pointless to dive.

"Wave, wave, just wave!"

One man understands: "If we were really Frenchmen, then let's do it right!"

Caps and arms swing in the air, handkerchiefs are only sparsely represented, and one of them is even willing to utter a would-be French-sounding word.

At 20 meters' altitude the plane comes at us.

And sure enough . . . he waves with one hand, then the engine roars and he disappears again toward Corfu.

We all look at one another.

Then one bursts out laughing loudly and soon everyone else is doubling up.

Müller laughs: "Sir, it is a good thing we haven't yet rebuilt! In the end, waving alone might not have fooled him!"

In Santa Quaranta we find only a Greek steamer. We continue our search.

Out to sea from Corfu, an antediluvian warship comes in sight, accompanied by six torpedo boats.

"Hey, look at that one!"

"If an old crate like that has such an escort, he must at least be loaded with gold or there is some big shot on board."

We cannot follow through on the attack. The ships come about suddenly and *U-14* is shaken off. Later they come about again. Then *U-14* realizes the enemy has thought of a new defense against U-boats: a zigzag course.

"Yes, when they move like that, we, too, must attack differently. At least we know about it for the next time."

A couple of days later the following message is decoded: General Kitchener coming from Patras accompanied by six torpedo boats arrived safe and sound in Brindisi.

Then it dawns on the men of *U-14* and we sincerely regret the "safe and sound."

Both engines have broken down, so *U-14* lands in the Drin Gulf after a few days of fruitless scouting and settles overnight on the bottom so the engines can be repaired and left as undisturbed as possible.

In the morning after surfacing, all are on deck. The men are spread over the whole deck, leaning anywhere and enjoying the morning sun.

The only thing that distinguishes the *Curie* externally from her French U-boat sisters is the steering blade of the vertical steering. It is beautifully painted, with wavy lines as a mark of recognition for Austrian U-boats.

At this moment a couple of men are standing in front of it, rolling their morning cigarettes.

According to custom, the flag is not flown.

"Periscope portside!"

In the calm water from 200 meters' distance a periscope comes toward the boat.

"Both engines full speed forward—sharp starboard—emergency dive!"

The maneuver goes very swiftly this time, but it is still too slow for me. How could I have let myself be so surprised? At any moment a torpedo could come.

Everyone in the boat sighs with relief as 12 meters' depth is reached.

Then we go again on the lookout.

"What do you know—our *U-11*!" I grumble. "What did he frighten us for?"

"Surface and take it easy!"

U-11 lies on the surface of the water and the men peer out curiously from the other side.

"Scoundrel, what kind of stupid joke are you playing?" I greet my friend.

"Well, I came a hair's breadth away from sinking you! I had my finger on the firing knob and Riegele kept urging, 'Why don't you fire? Such a chance will never come again!'"

"Yes, but didn't you recognize me?"

"No, your men stood in front of the steering blade and only when you gave the alarm and they moved did I see the wavy lines. Just think. Last night an English ship lay aground, too! Three of us slept here!"

"Well, I am sorry to say, I must leave him to you; my engines are broken down once again. I'm going home. Have a good trip!"

En route, a sack of good Canadian flour is fished out of the water. A thin paste has formed around it from the seawater, but inside the flour is bone dry. For all, a much desired improvement for the mess.

That evening *U-14* limps in. One electric motor still runs. The other one's clutch gave out.

But at this point no one cares. Nothing can happen anymore; there is the harbor entrance. I am deeply grateful that we have come home this time unscathed. We can still steer, but that's about all. Practically everything else has broken down.

Then—am I seeing correctly? Has the man at the helm gone crazy? I stand powerlessly on the tower and watch as the boat swings around and races at full speed into the rows of our own mines, which are anchored here at a depth of only 2 meters.

Before I can fully grasp the horror of the situation, *U-14* has already gone through them in a wide arc, and the mines are left behind.

This time all the guardian angels must have helped together! So, now the rudder is broken, too. At 10 degrees to port in the narrow mine passage it gets stuck and lets the boat travel full speed through her own mines.

"By the way, the reconstruction!" I say as we disembark. "Vio, you are the best technician of all of us; you can work out the request for the proposed repairs!"

Nineteen. Bypassing the Official Channels

The requested rebuilding has been granted. *U-14* has hardly arrived in Pola when I am ordered to the fleet command so I can personally explain my requests.

An entire board of inquiry convenes to judge my petitions. None of those present has actually been on a U-boat, except possibly on a short peacetime trip. But I find complete sympathy for my suggestions.

Everything is agreed to, except for the cannon I requested. I insist on an 8.8-centimeter cannon. It shoots much farther than the 65-mm Skoda normally allocated and is the strongest caliber that the boat can endure. Naturally its effect is something completely different.

The ordnance officer hesitates: "An unusual caliber! Where are you going to get the ammunition for it? This has never happened yet! To make an exception for a U-boat! How can a new cannon be inventoried?"

I see no difficulties. I have already spoken with the German U-boat station. I can get as much ammunition as I want; also, we are at war, and the cannons are there to shoot and not for inventory.

Fig. 16. Setting torpedoes in the harbor

"Well, we'll see."

U-14 lies at Olive Island in Pola. The shipyard workers pour into the boat and rip everything out. The only thing left is the empty hull.

The engines go to Graz where new diesels are manufactured at the railroad car factory. In Graz, machinist mate Mayerhofer has to demonstrate the engine once more. He who had cursed the old thing so often because it caused him so much work, irritation, anxiety, sleepless nights, and ruined Sundays. He is as happy as a child.

So he lets the dismantled engine be moved into the factory and assembles it there.

"Just you wait, you . . ." he murmurs and is full of vengeful thoughts. The mere idea that he should demonstrate it again for a trial angers him. So there are still men who think in all seriousness that there could be something left to repair or to patch on this engine . . . ? But he knows that this will be its swan song.

Fig. 17. A Russian provision ship captured during the war

As soon as he is finished, the committee appears. Mayerhofer turns on the engine only to half speed. Why, the engine "runs like clockwork!" He lets it run faster, and soon he hears the well-known rumble, the irregular surges that he knows only too well. This noise had often woken him out of many a deep sleep. And he almost thinks he hears the voice of his commander: "Mayerhofer, your equipment is breaking down again!"

He lets the engine run faster and faster, respectfully asks the committee to move back a few steps as a precaution, and finally switches it to full speed.

On board he never would have dared do that, but he has been looking forward to this moment for hours.

A rumble goes through the engine, a coughing . . . a crash . . . and pieces fall off.

"I am completely amazed at how long you have been able to make this thing run!" says the committee's director, full of sincere appreciation for him.

Mayerhofer has survived his test. The engine was really ready for scrap iron.

A conning tower is cast at the Skoda works, new steel plates come from Witkowitz, and parts that the sea arsenal cannot manufacture by itself arrive from all regions of the monarchy.

It is now time to think of the cannon's pedestal. In the arsenal they talk of a 65-mm Skoda cannon; they have already drafted the diagrams for it and the work must begin soon.

I fear the worst. I have not yet received a decision. I get impatient and want to speak with my superior, but it is full moon and my superior is on an official visit to some factory.

My representative is not informed. So I sit down and write the cannon factory in Germany. I want to know the price and delivery time for my cannon.

I wait for a reply. It takes a long time; then it comes from an unexpected place.

"The Captain should come immediately to the flagship," a telephone order advises.

"All the while we've had to rush and all the while we have waited," I think to myself and go over.

I first seek out my old friend, the admiral. Before you go into the lion's den, it is better to know what it is all about.

"Hello, what do you want from me?"

"But what did you start up? The ordnance expert spits when he hears your name!"

"What's his problem? Did I step on his corns?"

"Ha, don't fool around! You . . . this is dreadful; you ordered a cannon. Without asking. By detouring the official channels."

"Naturally! For four months they keep me waiting and you do nothing. In the arsenal they are talking about a Skoda that I don't really want. So I wrote them myself. I'm the one going out there, not you! How did they find out about this?"

"Because of suspicions of espionage, the factory couldn't answer directly and so they referred the request to the Fleet."

"Well, I'll just have to go to Haus.[1] I must have my cannon."

"Well, you won't succeed that way. Haus will ask his expert and he is flatly against it. Especially now."

I try my luck with the fleet commander. Always the same: I cannot get around the ordnance expert.

Only through official channels, if possible with your reservation number!

"So, I will go to the old grouch myself!" I finally go and am announced.

I am received politely with an ice-cold stare.

"Sir, I came on account of my cannon," I blurt out.

"Yes, you ordered yourself a cannon without going through official channels! By evading me personally! What you have dared to do is unheard of! You will not receive your cannon!"

"Sir, for four months now I have requested the cannon; until now nothing has happened. The boat is ready and the cannon must be installed now. So I finally took matters into my own hands!"

"And now you think you can force the cannon out of me. You will get a Skoda. To simply bypass me . . ."

The outraged one is not about to change his mind.

"Holy crow, be diplomatic just once . . . I must have my cannon!" I think to myself, and suddenly I get inspired.

"Sir, I didn't even think of detouring you personally! I can make no requests without first doing some research. I only wanted to know when the cannon could be delivered and how much it would cost. Only then I would have presented you with my proposal and naturally would leave it to your judgment to grant it or not."

"Oh, that puts a new perspective on things! You really did not mean to evade me personally?"

"No sir, there was never any question of that."

"Well, let me think about it." And I am dismissed in a somewhat more friendly fashion.

Fourteen days later the cannon arrives.

Twenty. Unrestricted U-Boat War

On January 1, 1917, Austro-Hungarian and German U-boat officers sit together in the officers' club in Pola.

News arrives to everybody's relief: Germany has declared unrestricted U-boat war.

"Thank God, they have finally understood. But it is rather late!"

"Of course, now that they don't know any more what's what; we are supposed to win the war at the last minute. God only knows what's going on. For a whole year we are supposed to do absolutely nothing, and now everything is supposed to go fast, fast."

"And how lovely that they have given the Allies plenty of time to prepare. Now the defense looks quite different from what it did a year ago. Then it would have been faster and easier. Now they say we are supposed to sink 600,000 tons a month; then England will be done for by autumn. . . . That's been statistically and accurately calculated!"

"They should go jump in a lake with their statistics! What do they know about how many ships England has added and how many are under construction in America! We'll 'manage,' but leave me alone with those statistics—how many boats do you have in Germany?"

"There are many still under construction. We have enough to handle the whole thing."

"Naturally, we cannot ferret out of you how many boats you have. But you are right; no one needs to know that. This place is full of spies."

"If only they would build them at home in Austria, too!"

"But I can tell you this: in Germany they are working. The whole industry is geared to U-boats. They are launching one after the other. Instead of typewriters and sewing machines, torpedoes are made in the factories. Everything works that way.

"It's a pity about the lost time because now we have to make up what we missed in more than a year."

"Now the United States will also declare war!"

"Yes, and also Nicaragua and San Marino. The world is in a fine state!"

"You know, Bethmann-Hollweg was to blame for more than he probably knows! He always gave in and constantly showed only weakness . . . and oh, don't hurt the enemy! That only strengthened and encouraged the enemy. When you feel weak and let the enemy know that, you cannot enforce peace. And he has always done it this way."

"But now, tell me this, why hasn't he been dumped since everyone knows this?"

The other shrugs his shoulders. "But now it does not matter any more, and we got our U-boat war!"

"Fine, but do you know why we finally have it? Because the Supreme Command is not confident any more of a victory by land. The U-boat war is their last hope!"

"But you won't give up?"

"Not I; that will be taken care of by those in the interior, yours and ours. Everything has been poisoned already. They have had nothing to eat for a long time . . .

"But let's not be angry today! How does that beautiful song go? 'Because it was in springtime . . .'"

"Hi kids, I'm buying the tenth bottle. Who will share it with me?"

Twenty-One. Reconstruction in the Arsenal

On full moon nights Italian planes fly to Pola. They are usually detected during their approach to the coast from the north because their clatter can be heard from afar, and forts and ships can be warned. But sometimes they appear by surprise from the sea in a glide.

In Pola no lights burn, even on the darkest nights. All windows must be shut tightly and on the streets you must grope around

Fig. 18. Sinking steamer

with your saber so as not to run into something. Soon flashlights are sold out; they have to be covered with red paper when on so that their bright light does not betray the person using one.

Spies are suspected everywhere: those who could give signals from the skylights toward the sky, and overzealous patrols shoot into many a window where an accidental light beam made its way.

But the planes come during daytime, too, and the house owners outside the city are encouraged to paint camouflage designs on their houses to resemble forests. The most beautiful patterns are recommended, and soon you can also see the most peculiar paintings on vacant houses.

The families of navy men have been exiled from Pola since the beginning of the war, and only those women who perform the difficult duty of nursing the sick are permitted to remain.

The air attacks are repeated often. The damage is trifling and

Fig. 19. S.M.U. *14* in the Mediterranean, with crewmembers

soon I worry less about my boat that is still being rebuilt. The last details seem to drag on forever.

I am getting impatient. The Mediterranean beckons with her transport steamers, so much the more inviting since now there are no more restrictions. And I want to arrive in good time for the final effort.

RECONSTRUCTION IN THE ARSENAL

Then I am asked "affectionately" if my boat will be ready soon, especially by those who have been moored for years.

But the work is actually delayed. It is quite similar to Penelope's tapestry: mysterious forces impede the construction.[1] The crew is suspicious.

There are many Czechs in the arsenal known to be capable of sabotage. In the mess they always sit together and speak Czech and every time a setback occurs on the front, their faces beam. At the American declaration of war, they supposedly really celebrated, but you can't pin anything on them.

Therefore, everything on the boat must be supervised and the crew personally inspects all the work because they only trust themselves.

The officers in the arsenal run from one workshop to another, in order to expedite the activity there, and I make a whirlwind tour through the various offices. The engineers assigned to the boat do their best, and when U-14 is finally ready to go for her first trial run, I congratulate them, as they have really performed outstandingly.

In their own way, the French had invented and manufactured this boat brilliantly, but only our thoroughness made a warship out of it that can do more than just go underwater.

A couple of weeks later U-14 steers toward the Strait of Otranto en route to the Mediterranean.

When we see the French airplanes, we know they are coming to protect the Strait of Otranto. They use proven tactics to come from the direction of the sun. Sometimes also torpedo boats force the boat to go underwater in a hurry; she must also tolerate bombs. This is very good training for the new crew, who can now show what they learned during the short trial runs.

Then the actual submarine blockade comes, and the passage through it marked by groups of fishing trawlers. These have come over from England and are supposed to carry out their normal trade, dragging nets. Only they deal with different nets and different fish.

These trawlers, as they call themselves, scour the navigable water in wide formations day in, day out, and try to make life difficult for the U-boats.

It must be an aggravating and boring tour of duty on board there. To search perpetually for periscopes and to have to lie there in all kinds of weather with their lowered nets . . . and then seldom to have the change of a catch of "fish." And yet they have succeeded several times . . . because several boats are lying on the bottom of the Strait of Otranto.

On *U-14* we are on the sharpest lookout as usual. Now we are the prey and the vessels that prowl around, the hunters. Granted, tired, weary hunters who have become dull from the long hunt day and night.

We succeed in avoiding the trawlers' masts, which rise above the horizon, and after a couple of hours the blockade lies behind our boat.

Finally we reach our actual goal, the Mediterranean, the Promised Land of the U-boats.

Twenty-Two. The First Steamers

It is April, the most beautiful season in the South.

During this season in peacetime, the pleasure steamers pass through all the Mediterranean harbors, and swarms of happy people pour over onto the sunny land to drink in the sun, the warmth, and the sea.

Rome, Naples, the Balearic Islands, Tunis, Morocco, Athens, Constantinople, Alexandria! Enticing posters with mosques, camels, Vesuvius, the Acropolis, beautiful blacks carrying amphorae, Aetna, and the pyramids usually entice the northerners to shorten the winter and to spend Easter, the joyful time, at the birthplace of culture.

On the U-boat we can no longer recall peacetime.

It must be nice to be carefree, to pass other steamers and to wave back and forth without having to look for periscopes. To arrive in harbors greeted by twenty-one gun salutes and to be greeted joyfully by other nations who strive to show off and to display their harbors in the best light.

In peacetime . . . it must be like being in a fairy-tale land.

Besides, everything that the people look for at Easter time in the South is still there now. Why is war actually being waged? Afterward, will it be more beautiful in the world?

The two islands of Cerigo and Cerigotto in Greece lie between Crete and Cape Matapan.[1] All steamers that want to go to Salonika to supply the French troops there must come through here. These islands become footholds, so to speak, of enemy destroyers and U-boat hunters who guard the straits.

West of these islands *U-14* cruises slowly back and forth looking for smoke.

In the meantime the steamers have learned how to travel without smoke, and only occasionally a small cloud from the cleaning of the boiler firebox will betray a faraway steamer.

For days on end our boat lies there, and it seems as if the enemy avoids this region. Nothing comes in sight and I think gradually of moving on.

Life on board is monotonous and the crew whiles away the time as best they can. The boat's band competes with the gramophone and a gymnastics club, which proudly performs on deck.

The gunnery petty officer, in civilian life a window cleaner from Berlin, plays the mouth organ wonderfully and attempts to lead songs with three such mouth organs, modulating in all keys and even accompanying with "m-ta-ta."

Previously sharks were seldom seen in the Mediterranean. Now they apparently have increased a lot and stay around, and as long as people swim, a lookout stands ready with a rifle. Even a swordfish stays in the vicinity of the boat. Every now and then he jumps high out of the water, the drops of water fall from his long sword; then he smacks down on the water and disappears.

Finally one evening the first steamer approaches. He appears to be coming from the Strait of Messina and steers toward Cape Matapan. All alone, without escort.

The attack is child's play. In the darkness my periscope is not visible; calmly, I can let my quarry enter my line of sight, and the torpedo strikes midship.

The steamer stays there and soon through the periscope you can see the life boats hurrying under sail toward land into a fresh northwest wind. The full moon shines in the sky and against its light the 12-centimeter gun is distinctly visible on deck. The gun crew could still be ready, so our boat moves into the dead zone of the enemy gun, surfaces, and begins to shoot at the waterline. The shell explosions ring back like echoes and a stream flows from the bullet holes; it appears to be grain.

The steamer stays afloat for hours, for the air cannot escape upward through the sealed cargo space, until finally the hatches break open and then it is too bad that you cannot photograph at night.

The moon is behind the steamer. It is a magnificent scene—the ship, as if it were a mortally wounded wild animal, rears up for the last time, lifts the bow steeply out of the water, stands still a moment, and then sinks perpendicularly into the deep.

The first 6,000 tons have been sunk.

A few days later the first convoy comes into view. The steamers go in two columns, three in the right column, two in the left, the biggest one leads. The fishing trawlers protect them on both sides.

This technique is not new at all. At the time of Philip II, the Spaniards' silver ships leaving America were caught by pirates or were captured by English privateers; in their distress they came up with the idea to sail in a convoy. The valuable ships were escorted by warships, "convoyed."

In the course of time pirates died out and this type of defense fell into oblivion.

Suddenly the U-boats came, the most dreadful pirates of all time. And then the steamers travel just like the silver ships of times past. They don't risk going alone anymore and select the old established means, the convoy.

U-14 has an opportune position on the steamers' course and steers in front of them out of sight. I know all the newest tricks of the convoys, how they want to deceive U-boats by zigzagging. Now I want to find out what kind of zigs and zags they will take. It is assumed that the pilot of this convoy is not constantly standing on the bridge, but that the change of course has been established from the beginning according to a schedule. I rely on that and after an hour I realize that every fifteen minutes the course is altered 20 degrees. Once to starboard, then to port. I have also ascertained the enemy's speed, and I need this information in order to know how far ahead I must aim my torpedo.

In total peace and quiet the boat goes underwater while I plan my attack. My target is the biggest steamer, and I consider: the fishing trawlers protect both outer sides, so I would be least disturbed between the two columns. I adjust my speed so that I can steer between the two columns after the steamers have come about; then the broadside torpedoes should come into operation.

It is a ticklish feeling to approach a ship from the front. A bow like that could cut through a U-boat as if it were butter; we must not be seen and barely, but at the right moment, look out.

"Torpedo three ready!"

Torpedo three lies in the swivel apparatus to starboard. Fastened aft next to the steering crossbar it gets a little thrust at the right moment, veers out under its own power, and is released as soon as it is on target.

U-14 moves very close alongside one of the columns. In the periscope you can see only the dark hull of the first ship sliding by. The men on the steamer could throw bombs and hand grenades with their hands onto our boat. I pull the periscope quickly around. The big steamer should come in line to starboard, and the compass readings shift very quickly now according to the movement of the target.

Another quick look to port to see what the next steamer in line is doing. But this one is already sending the alarm. The typical white steam puffs escape from the steam pipe at the stack and the steamer veers to ram our U-boat.

The bow moves alarmingly and sharply through the water directly at the periscope, pushing a wide wake before it. Only 300 meters separate the two vessels approaching each other.

"Now act fast," I tell myself and bring the periscope around. I do not want to let the steamer go but want to torpedo it quickly before I evade the impact.

It is still barely possible; the big steamer is just entering the sights. One more glance at the dangerous edge of the bow, which is already menacingly close, then back again to the steamer.

"Torpedo three, fire! Quick dive to 20 meters! Pull in the periscope!"

Straining, all those on board listen.

Ten, twenty, thirty seconds. Nothing, no explosion that would indicate a direct hit.

It had been such a sure shot!

"Dammit, Laudon, what went wrong?" I cannot find a curse juicy enough for my frustration. Also, I do not have time because the second steamer is passing over us, and we hear the "Sssst, sssst, sssst" of the propellers above the boat. All of a sudden it's over.

"Periscope!"

Unperturbed, the big steamer has continued on and can no longer be reached. But maybe we can get the next one, to port.

"All starboard! Torpedo seven ready!"

Our boat must go in a complete circle and can send its torpedo just after the last steamer. The explosion climbs toward the sky between the ship's hold and engines, a dark cloud mixed with white steam. Boiler explosion.

The trawlers have no time to worry about the U-boat since both must come to the aid of the visibly sinking ship.

Confusion reigns. Lifeboats are hastily launched, bundles and crates come sailing over the railing into them, and men jump into the tipping boats. One of them capsizes and lines are thrown to the swimmers from the trawlers.

The steamer becomes smaller and smaller. She sinks horizontally until only a thin streak remains, on which the masts stand. Then these also smack the water.

U-14 takes off underwater from the scene of action.

Now I have the time to vent my feelings.

"What went wrong with torpedo three? Did it fire at all?"

The torpedo officer had already examined everything. Everything in the boat had gone in order; the defect must lie externally. Now I am really angry.

I can't even find anyone on whom to cool my rage and must swallow it myself.

I throw myself on my berth.

Such a big steamer—and to lose it! Nearly rammed and then everything was in vain! Some flaw in the equipment caused by an unknown someone who will take no responsibility for what his negligence caused.

I work myself more and more into a rage.

Then suddenly I am overwhelmed with astonishment—I can't believe myself. How could I have worked myself into such a destructive frame of mind?

It is exactly one year since I sank the *Léon Gambetta*; I can well remember how I had felt then.

But . . . during this past year much has changed. I have been home on leave. There I watched my children eat beetroot; meat, vegetables, butter, and eggs are not even talked about anymore. I heard that gypsum was mixed into the flour for bread and that supposedly coffee was made of roasted May beetles. When you had to eat the stuff, you could almost believe it. I had seen women who couldn't nurse their own children because they themselves had nothing more to eat, and children, even very small ones, who had to be fed with a substitute tea.

And how is this supposed to continue?

Today I would not have any scruples about sinking my first cruiser. Since my leave I understand what the enemy means by "war"—annihilation. And the whole future generation would be annihilated with it!

Knowing this, shouldn't I have the fiercest desire to destroy?

But it has now also become a sport. Before the war I collected stamps; now I collect sunken tonnage.

It is a fine hunt after all! The game is: defend yourself now; and we do so with more fury. Today it was still a joke, but the enemy supposedly has bombs now that can blast a hole in the side of a boat from 50 meters.

Yes, yes, I have lost compassion for the drowning enemy; he has none either.

I return to reality. I throw off my thoughts and step to the periscope.

I am now 6,000 meters away from the steamers. We surface and follow after them. I still want to overtake them to get the big steamer.

The fishing trawlers that had stayed behind come up and intercept me and open fire. But not for long because the hard-won 8.8-centimeter cannon reaches farther and now the trawlers seek protection from behind the armed steamers.

In the afternoon the visibility becomes poor. The horizon becomes hazy; in the mist the convoy changes direction and is lost to us.

Twenty-Three. Transmission of Orders

The chase has brought *U-14* so far west that I decide to continue on toward the nearby Strait of Messina.

During the night our boat arrives there.

The beacons shine as in peacetime and it is easy to get my bearings. In the shadows cast by the mountains on the mainland, the boat steers farther in toward the narrows. It is perfectly calm. Only the muffled sound of the engines echoes from the steep coast. The tanks are partly flooded so that we can dive quickly.

At any moment we expect the bright beam of a searchlight or the fire from a shore battery.

But apparently the war has not yet reached here.

Before dawn the boat dives in order to cruise underwater in front of Messina.

There in the morning the beach becomes full of life. Beach chairs and colorful tents are set up, brightly dressed women stroll along with parasols, and with a bit of imagination, you could even hear the band that you can see there.

Surely someone is hawking, "Gelato!"

"Scheure, look at that! Don't you feel like a little goulash, a fresh roll, and a mug of beer?"

The navigator looks out.

"Sir, is this for real? I think they wash themselves every day with fresh water!

"And look at all the girls!"

The others have to look through the periscope, too.

"Such a pretty sight! It seems to me they don't even feel the war. But I'd like to see them run if we were to surface suddenly!!"

Then we look at one another: unwashed, unkempt, hands all greasy with oil . . .

"Men, we have to shave for a change. Look at us! If my mother could see this!"

We have been at sea fourteen days and have used fresh water sparingly.

Now, for once, everyone should have a chance to really wash. Two liters per person are doled out. You must learn how to get clean with so little water.

Afterward, all the faces shine . . . most unusual!

Even fresh shirts are put on!

Only the girls are to blame for the magic of this cleanliness; they sit sunning themselves out there in the sand, unsuspecting that their pleasant influence has reached underwater.

But *U-14* did not go to Messina because of the beach, and she must search elsewhere.

A couple of small torpedo boats that are probably on sentry duty are uninteresting. It would be a pity to waste a shot. Otherwise there is no traffic. Only a small steamer, accompanied by an armed yacht and a torpedo boat, has come within range.

At the attack *U-14* has to dive under the yacht and come back up just in time; everything is ready for "torpedo fire" . . . and again the torpedo doesn't go off!

This time we catch him: the culprit who is guilty of forgetting to release the torpedo. Everyone is indignant.

"Son of a bitch and a black pot!" swears the cook softly amid his pots and pans.

The unlucky one had come on board only fourteen days before and did not yet know U-boat customs. He did not comprehend that all instructions must be repeated. Also the commands. So that no error could possibly be made.

With the U-boat recruit by his side, the second officer stands forward in the engine room.

"Machinist mate, report!" He climbs out of his engine hole. "Your order?"

"Mayerhofer, take this one here! He didn't clear the torpedo at all; he says he didn't understand and only said 'Yes!' each time to say something.

"Now make him understand that he must repeat every command and also that everything he reports through the megaphone must be repeated to him."

"Yes!" and then to the man: "So young man, now come on over here! Hasn't it gotten through your thick head yet that here on board everything is repeated? Now because of you we lost 3,000 tons again!

"Now—you stay here by the megaphone and repeat every order I give you. Understand?"

Mayherhofer goes into the control room and calls into the megaphone: "Wet the launching apparatus!"

"Yes!"

"Not 'Yes'—you should repeat!"

"Yes!"

Mayerhofer gets scared. The man is apt to execute the order. He springs forward and catches him just in time.

"You blockhead, don't you understand that this is just verbal practice? That you are learning the transmission of orders but must not carry out any? What language do you really speak?"

"Please, I am Czech."

"Oh, that, too! Now look here," then the schooling continues.

"Open the flood valves!" (Nothing can happen there; they are open anyway.)

"Yes!"

"For God's sake, you shouldn't answer 'Yes!' Do you understand?"

"Yes!"

"You hopeless idiot—repeat it!"

"Please, should I repeat that, too?"

Twenty-Four. Fog

U-14 charges her batteries farther out at sea overnight and then cruises along the Sicilian coast.

Between Cape Passero and Cape Murro di Porco steamer traffic has been established along the coast and sure enough, a steamer shows up that is staying close to land and traveling north. During the chase a thick fog rolls in from the coast, breaking from time to time, just enough to maintain contact with the ship.

But before *U-14* has reached an area where the enemy is close by, the fog thickens and the voyage goes into the unknown.

Suddenly a dark speck appears out of the fog and develops into a small island that lies in the water like a stone. I consult the chart. For the first time after a blind trip of many hours, ori-

Fig. 20. A torpedo hit

entation is possible. It is one of the stones that old Polyphemus
threw after Odysseus.

The steamer also cannot go closer to land, so the U-boat stops
and waits.

Suddenly someone points upward.

The fog has lightened and high above us a vision appears that
at first seems ghostly. In the air, almost at the zenith, a snow-
covered mountaintop hovers.

It is Mount Aetna that looks out calmly and majestically.[1] It
has seen much in the course of centuries; it has made and experienced history. . . . But even for Aetna, a torpedoed steamer
would be a novelty.

I would have gladly furnished Aetna this spectacle, but the
pursued steamer has either taken off toward Catania or slipped
by in the fog.

A bewitched region! There—like the spectral fingers of a

Fig. 21. Shipwrecked seamen amid the wreckage of a sunken steamer

hand that reaches upward ominously toward Aetna! After a longer look we solve the puzzle. The "fingers" are the smokestacks of a factory that is not aware of how the fingers of the U-boat crew itch to send off a couple of shells into it.

But *U-14* will not stoop to something like that.

The next day brings more fog!

A U-boat is dependent on far and clear vision, so there is no weather she hates more than this.

Suddenly a small patrolling torpedo boat appears.

"Emergency dive!"

The tower is scarcely awash when a flood of water pours in around the hatch. All efforts to make it watertight are useless and more water streams in. The boat must surface immediately, after the enemy has vanished in the fog.

It turns out that the rubber seal could no longer stand up to the heat and pressure and has begun to crumble, and there is no spare on board. So, take out the caulking and rewrap it with insulating tape.

"But quickly, quickly, before the torpedo boat comes back!" During the repair our boat cannot submerge and is helpless.

Three men go to work. In the damp air the sound penetrates much too far; we have to be careful. The boat lies stopped; the men whisper.

I start to get impatient; the work is going far too slowly. If we had to dive right now, I could shut the hatch that leads from the tower into the boat and let the tower fill with water. The damage this would cause could not be repaired at sea.

Finally the wrapping is finished.

But . . . now the rubber seal will not fit into its groove. A section of it has hardly been pressed in when it pops out again as the rest is worked in.

I stand on pins and needles.

Then next to me I hear the command, "Pronto" and then more inarticulate words.

The torpedo boat must be very close, but where is it going? On our U-boat everyone freezes. No one moves. The men at the conning tower automatically duck like rabbits in a furrow.

Then we hear splashing around our boat, the other's bow wake hits our boat . . . noises move away . . . it is quiet again.

The danger has passed.

The fog stands like a white wall—but this time it is blessed by all the men on *U-14*.

"So, now hurry up, will you?" the innocent are urged on. But it takes quite some time before they can finish their painstaking work and the hatch can be shut.

Twenty-Five. The Two Greeks

This foggy land is no place for a U-boat, and *U-14* steers slowly and carefully to her original hunting territory, Cape Matapan.

On the way we meet one steamer traveling singly, and I shoot a torpedo . . . and miss.

This time I rake myself over the coals and would like to box my own ears in front of a mirror, but I don't have one.

For days nothing comes into view.

Then the lookout reports a sail under Cape Matapan that is heading from Cape Sapienza toward land.

Finally a change in the tedious life on board.

Immediately I challenge the schooner to heave to with a gunshot. But she does not respond and flees farther toward land. A second shot is impossible because the counter-recoil mechanism is broken. So we haul up the machine gun.

U-14 travels full speed; I want to cut off the sailboat from land before he comes into Greek territorial waters.

I stop short.

"Are we at war with Greece?"

No one knows.

Lately, from all parts of the world, declarations of war have come flying in.

Some come from countries that could never think of engaging in the war and are only out to seize freighters that had fled into their previously neutral harbors. Others might have been pressured by the Central Powers. Whether Greece was among those no one knows.

I inquire throughout the boat. No one remembers having heard about it.

But for the present the sailboat is still two miles from land and is consequently outside the territorial waters.

A couple of shots from the machine gun cause the captain to raise his hands in surrender, but he still moves right along. Only a second salvo induces him to heave to and let the sails luff. He bears the Greek flag and understands enough Italian that he puts a boat into the water and comes over.

Already from afar he waves something that close at hand turns out to be a beautiful old icon. Now we can see only the silver frame glinting in the sun.

At the same time, he calls loudly as if to confirm, "Long live Austria! Long live Austria!"

Then he jumps on board, runs aft to kiss the red, white, and red flag, comes with many bows to the conning tower, and gushes about his solemn declaration, "Long live Constantine, long live Constantine, not Venizelos!"

He means Constantine, the king of Greece, whose words carry no weight because he is no longer able to effectively oppose Venizelos, the war instigator—so the captain is declaring his loyalty to the peace-loving party. He rejects any blame for an eventual declaration of war.

There he stands, tanned, slight, in a shabby gray civilian suit, an expression half sly, half frightened in his sharply etched face, and talks uninterruptedly. And as his Italian is sorely lacking, he uses his hands and feet to help as he protests and assures.

Then he puts his hand in his breast pocket and pulls out photographs. Where on earth did he get these? Franz Joseph, Conrad von Hötzendorf, the German Emperor, Hindenburg . . . a whole pack of famous men from the Central Powers.

"Sir, on the other side he probably had Poincaré, Grey, and his associates," says Scheure. "Just look at him; this is a real Grego!"

But at such a boat inspection you could catch lice.

The sailboat comes from Calamata with raisins for Piraeus.

A beautiful schooner, with such fine lines! With her fine tall white sails luffing in the light breeze she resembles an enticing fairy that is inviting the rough U-boat companions to continue farther with her into the realm of the many islands. Where once Odysseus got lost and then couldn't tear himself away. Farther into the East where men smoke Tschibuk with their black coffee and have acquired or kept enough wisdom—that for them time has not yet become money. Into the land of a thousand and one nights . . .

I keep looking to the schooner where my men are waiting to blow up the ship.

"A fine ark, that. It would be a shame to sink the beautiful sailboat. He can do us no harm. Let him go!"

And over to the schooner: "Hello! Throw the deck cargo overboard, don't blow up the ship!"

And now sacks of raisins fly overboard. The Greeks have to help, much as they would have liked to duck out. Then the hold is ripped open. Everything is full of raisins! Loose raisins! Enough for a million *gugelhupfs*![1] But how can we get them out? It would be well into the night before we could shovel out the hold. In the meantime, the two vessels have drifted farther toward land and have come into Greek territorial waters.

"Oh well, let our men come back, but they should bring back a sack of raisins with them. They should have a treat, too, for once. We'll let the Greek go!"

The captain has been standing by sadly; he cannot understand the German commands. He watches dejectedly as his cargo goes overboard. He says nothing more, and only stares at his beautiful ship, which he already considers lost.

But now, although he doesn't understand a word of German, he suddenly understands. Whether it was the tone of my voice, whether it was the different expression on the men's faces . . . in a flash he comprehends: not only has the ship been given to him, but he may also bring home part of the cargo. The expressive face with the agile eyes shines with joy. And now the most heartfelt good wishes flow from his lips just as the curses for Venizelos had moments before. He takes his leave with many bows.

In the meantime the sailboat's dinghy has come alongside with the export duty of a sack of raisins and a gigantic stalk of bananas, a most welcome improvement to the mess after endless canned goods!

The schooner hauls in the sheets, the sails fill with the light wind, and once again her name sparkles in the sun, *Ephtuphia*. Then she continues on her course toward Cape Matapan.

"One good deed deserves another," I think, as on the following night we sink a freighter. He came straight toward me, practically ran into my arms.

From the boats that sheltered the shipwrecked, I search out the captain and have him come to the tower.

He is an older man, squat, a bit clumsy, with a brown leathery face and eyes that you can tell are used to looking into the far distance . . . so he stands there with his hat in his hand, his thin gray hair flying in the wind. He is also a Greek, but one of the older generation.

His steamer *Marionga Gulandris* has been in transit from Baltimore, Maryland, with 4,500 tons of wheat. On the entire long trip nothing has happened to him, and now, a couple of hours from his destination, bad luck caught up with him. It's tough, but after all, that is war.

Pain at the loss of his ship has overcome the old man. With twitching lips he wants to say something but he cannot get a word out. I want to console him as well as I can, give him a cigarette, have cognac brought from the medicine cabinet. . . . But what is wrong? It's suddenly getting very dark! Already one of the men points to the sky with a loud cry.

It is a clear, full moon night, with a stormy northwest wind. By the light of the moon you can see the sinking cargo ship over there struggling in the heavy seas; next to our U-boat the foreign captain's boat dances up and down and you can watch the worried, tense expressions in the faces of his men in detail. Suddenly we can see only dark, obscure shadows. No one has noticed how the moon has been increasingly obscured. A total lunar eclipse.

Now everyone is looking up with interest; only on the old captain does it make the least impression. What does the moon matter when he has lost his ship? He makes use of the others' interest and takes another deep gulp from the bottle. Then he wants to know if it was a torpedo or an underwater cannon that sank him. He has heard that such things exist.

I am astonished at his naïveté and ask him if he has lost any men.

"Yes, a young man who was operating the engine. What did he, an innocent one, do to deserve being killed in the war?

"Who will take responsibility for the whole thing before God someday? Damn war!"

I pity the old man and do not take offense at his indignation.

But I must break off the conversation because floodlights from Cerigo are searching the water, and the usual destroyers are coming closer. They must have heard the explosion.

The captain is given the course to the next harbor on the map. On a reach, with the fresh aft wind, he could be at Crete with his two boats by the next morning.

He expresses thanks and wants to leave the ship. A high sea comes alongside; he misses the moment to jump into his dinghy, a wave lifts it up high, the bow of our U-boat dives deeply into the water, and the old captain vanishes for a moment in the dark waves.

One man, who had tied himself to the cannon, quickly reaches over, fortunately catches him, and helps him into his dinghy.

Only the round hat dances on the waves.

Twenty-Six. Salute to Africa

Near the North African coast *U-14* pursues a steamer. During the night we had torpedoed the ship; but he has kept enough buoyancy to continue on, his stern deep in the water.

It has taken hours for us to finally get within range, because one of our engines is damaged, and we can continue with the other one only with difficulty.

Now the sinking steamer has reached Derna, a small harbor in the Cyrenica.

So close to firing, I won't let him escape anymore. Here in the harbor he cannot give me the slip again.

U-14 comes ever closer.

On land everything seems to have died out. There is hardly a settlement to see because the white dunes that lie before the city completely conceal everything.

Suddenly we are fired on.

The battery is invisible, but, according to the shell splashes, it must have three guns. We shoot at random over the concealing dunes without being able to see the impact of our shots. Only one signal or radio station is visible on a knoll and we fire our cannon at this. Then another battery, halfway up the mountain behind the city, enters the fray, and right after a third one is noticeable on the mountain ridge with very obvious smoke.

I bless the impatience of the artillerymen who once again could not wait.

Well, that could have been a lovely situation in the harbor. They would have had easy play with us. As it is, their shots fall short. They are shooting short of the target and aren't even trying to adjust their aim so that their shots are always equally short as we slowly withdraw.

The men come up, one after another: "Sir, may I shoot once, too?" and the cannon is shared by all in the ranks so that the men can have their fun.

Then we discontinue firing. The invisible batteries cannot be struck and it makes no sense to destroy houses.

Twenty-Seven. One Comes, the Other Goes

U-14 has been at sea for thirty days.

The last torpedo has been fired and the fuel is running low, as is the fresh water. We must return home, repair all the minor damage, take on new torpedoes and fuel oil, and get ready for the next trip.

And now suddenly the sea comes to life, as if it were bewitched.

Smoke trails come in sight on all sides. Until now we would have gone after each sign of smoke, every masthead that would appear, but now we must avoid any encounter.

Before we enter the Strait of Otranto I double the watch. The normal milling crowd of fishing trawlers is expected there. We have to make big circles around them so as not to be detected.

But we meet up with no patrols. The trip continues; nothing appears. We have passed the mountains of Corfu already—the horizon is empty.

It is almost uncanny—as if it were totally deserted.

"Something must be going on as there is nothing to see here—have they made peace by any chance?"

Saseno, the island in front of Valona, is off to starboard at a 90-degree angle. No planes are coming from there.

The riddle becomes more unclear.

Where are those ever-present torpedo boats?

"Well, this suits us!"

And someone sings, "Let's go home, let's go home, it's high time, let's go home to our folks!"

And then everyone cleans himself up for land. Beards come off, and the last bit of fresh water is released for washing. We bring out the second uniforms, the *Tagskleider*, which had been taken along specifically for arrival in the harbor. It is astonishing what elegant company appears on deck.

One crewmember climbs up the tower and rolls a cigarette. Then he stands upwind of the two officers, who had already changed their uniforms, and puffs away.

"What disgusting stuff are you smoking?"

"Sir, we are out of everything; we have to smoke tea."

"Aha, and that's why you are blowing the foul smell into my nose!" The officer laughs and hands him his tobacco box: "Here, have something better, and when it's empty, bring me back my box."

The man disappears on deck and soon a group surrounds him, eagerly rolling cigarettes and casting sly looks toward the tower. Then the box is returned.

"Many thanks, sir."

"That's all right, you sly fox, but now go to the commander, and tell him that I sent you."

"Yes, sir."

Then the officer turns to his comrade:

"There we have it. The Fleet Command has to generously forego our tobacco rations, and now the crew has nothing left to smoke. There isn't even a crumb of tobacco left in the Bocche, and whoever can't get some from Montenegro has to chew gum. But we may buy war bonds."

Now we can hear Morse code from the telegraph cabin. The operator is reporting our imminent arrival as well as the number of tons sunk, and with that the first link with our homeland is established.

Homeland. First of all that means mail from home, plenty of fresh water for washing, clean clothes, fresh bread and meat, and, if we are lucky, some good cold beer.

The Lovčen range is the first land to appear. But it still takes hours before the mountains of the lower peninsula, which form the gulf, are discernible to the naked eye.

We have raised the flag, and it and the *U-14* banner wave joyfully in the wind. We steer toward Punta D'Ostro and are greeted by the garrison with three energetic "Hurrahs!"

This time we don't head for Rose, the former U-boat harbor. Everything has gotten too crowded there. We pass Rose and head for Gjenovič, the newly completed U-boat station, where we are moored between buoy and land.

On the dock, the crews of the U-boats present greet us new arrivals. We are burning with curiosity: "Hallo, what's new in the world? Have they made peace already?"

"Ha, what do you think? What makes you say that?"

"It looked like it near Otranto. The sea was empty, not a patrol in sight!"

"Of course you don't know anything yet. Horthy was down

there with *Novara*, *Helgoland*, and *Saida* and cleaned up the fishing trawlers.

"Bravo! Did he sink many?"

"Fourteen fishing trawlers were sunk; they brought back around seventy prisoners.

Csepel and *Balaton* sank an Italian destroyer and one or two transports and also disabled a destroyer."

"Did we lose anything?"

"No, nothing, but you should see the *Novara*! She has already gone to Pola for repairs. The main funnel was shot right through and you should see the mess on deck. The *Saida* had to tow her in."

"Horthy is wounded and Szuborits was killed."

"What, Bácsi?[1] Poor fellow. How did Horthy get wounded?"

"On his feet, badly, but things are supposed to be getting better."

"But with whom were they fighting? Can't you tell the story properly?"

"Well, as usual, with a bunch of British and Italian cruisers, and French and Italian destroyers. Murderously superior forces. A wonder that they came back at all! During the return they were cut off and fought their way through. At that moment the *Novara* lay disabled and was being taken in tow by the *Saida*. The enemy turned away and disappeared. It was a delicate maneuver, right in the middle of enemy fire. It is incredible that they broke off the fighting. They could have made mincemeat of our men. The *Sankt Georg* put out from the base with six units to help, but they were already gone."

"Now you will have a peaceful Otranto for a while. See all that is being done for you?"

"Oh yeah!" and everyone laughs.

Another U-boat is ready to go to sea. One of the officers comes over to me.

"Say, where did you find steamers?"

"Near Cerigo. On the route Cerigo-Malta, and Matapan-

Spartivento. Single steamships are rare—and armed. None carry a flag anymore. They don't travel in a direct course, but once to the south, then again to the north of the steamer's path in long zigzags in which they make more zigzags. The convoys are getting bigger and the escort is stronger. It is almost impossible to accomplish anything on the surface anymore. But someone hand me a cigarette; we ran out of tobacco!"

Five, six, cigarette boxes are offered me; then the officers of the departing U-boat take their leave. A shaking of hands, "have a good trip," and the commander of that boat goes on board last, where the crew awaits him at attention.

He accepts the report: "Boat and engines ready."

They cast off the lines, the U-boat maneuvers from the mooring, and at the command, "Position starboard," the free watch on deck mans the rail in salute, while the boat picks up speed and steers toward the passageway.

"See, there is always something going on around here!" says a sailor from the U-boat station who had been helping on the dock to another one: "One comes; the other goes!"

—The other goes!

He never returned.

Twenty-Eight. Gjenović

It has been more than a year since I was in the Bocche and everything has changed. With the increase in U-boats Rose could not provide enough room, and in Gjenović stone barracks were built, efficient workshops were set up, also supply depots and our own hospital. Motorboats are available and the former makeshift circumstances have ended. The U-boats, formerly stepchildren, have prevailed and equipment and money have been found for them.

We new arrivals now want to be alone. Alone with our mail. In thirty days a good pile should have accumulated!

Fig. 22. A cruiser flotilla pushes forward, toward Otranto

So every man withdraws into his quarters and reads and reads and forgets everything else around him.

Only then do we wash, that long foregone pleasure that we prolong and savor. A young girl getting ready for her first ball does not feel any more dressed up than a U-boat man who, after a long trip, puts on clean clothes once more.

But we are still on duty. The second officer has discussed thoroughly all the necessary repairs with the detail chiefs, and soon the work program is established; as soon as possible the boat must go out again.

The torpedo masters—the officers of the destroyers and torpedo boats—have built a pavilion on land, the "Gunners' Club," a sort of offshoot of the officers' casino in Pola. Here we can all sit together making plans and exchanging war stories.

We have often exchanged fire with the enemy and are far from novices at our military profession. Here you can learn more than from the official reports, and with the red Dalmatian wine the faces get flushed in the recollection of survived battles.

GJENOVIĆ

Fig. 23. A mine explosion

In the evening we officers of *U-14* are summoned and escorted to the Gunners' Club. We are greeted joyously; we must recount our stories, have a toast, and tell them again.

Then one speaks up: "Have you heard what happened to *U-4* the other day?"

"He had sunk a steamer in the Gulf of Tarento, and a sailing ship, when stormy weather blew in and he wanted to travel underwater for a night.

"They kept at twenty meters and the man at the diving rudder was pleased that he had steered the boat so well because the needle of the depth pressure gauge didn't move. He did not notice that its pipeline must have been blocked from the outside.

"Suddenly the bow dropped 25 degrees. Singule, the commander, was awakened in his bunk hearing the commands of his officers on watch. He dashed to the second depth gauge and read '60 meters.'

"U-4 was proven to 50 meters and the sinking did not stop.

"They wanted to blow out the tanks, but that didn't work. The air cylinders apparently could not stand up to the outside pressure. Singule wanted to steer the boat upward and ran with maximum power, but he couldn't prevent the sinking. It must have been a damnable state of affairs."

"And the *Fallkiel?*"[1]

"Yes, at 80 meters Singule had disengaged it. In any case, it is a miracle that it released at this angle.

"But the boat sank farther. At first the indicator hit 85 meters, the limit. Then something in the bow buckled, the paint peeled off and crackled down. It was clear that the boat's body must be giving way to the immense pressure.

"Well, everyone had crossed himself, giving up hope; then the first officer reported: 'Boat is ascending.' As if it had been an intended maneuver. After that they surfaced quickly.

"That Germania boat must have withstood over 100 meters' depth. No English or French boat could imitate that.

"But there he was, and between him and the Bocche was the blockade of Otranto, and he couldn't dive anymore because of the missing *Fallkiel*. It was as good as hopeless to think he could get through.

"Then the officers vowed a pilgrimage to Tersatto.

"And sure enough they were able to slip through, totally unseen!

"Just think, on the same day another was pushed underwater at Otranto eight times!

"What do you say to that?"

"Well, and have they been to Tersatto?"

"Of course! Naturally he had to go into Pola in dry dock and as he was unable to dive he had to skirt the coastline. But he stayed one day in Fiume and they went to Tersatto with burning candles. In uniform, naturally. Isn't that good?"

"Yes," added another, "And in Pola he was reprimanded because he had made the detour via Fiume! I don't think he told them about the pilgrimage."

"Such incredible luck . . . after all that bad luck!"

"And about the German—have you heard that already? He was lying underwater near Malta and let a steamer run over him that bent his periscope so badly he couldn't draw it in again.

"Well, he surfaced and while he lay there and recharged his battery, a plane came over from Malta. Naturally it was, 'Emergency dive!' and they forgot one man on deck! The plane was very close and the boat dove away under the man's feet. He scrambled high up on the crooked periscope and already could see himself swimming.

"Then they noticed in the boat that one man had been left on deck, and the captain was a good man and they didn't want to desert him. He surfaced, although surely the bombs would fall any minute. As the men opened the hatch, the plane turned away sharply, and they had an easy time letting the man in."

"And what had happened?"

"The bent periscope was aimed at the plane and with the man on top the whole thing must have looked like an antiaircraft gun and the pilot turned away!"

"Here's yet another story about a German.

"The Italians were at peace with Germany for an extra year

when we'd already been at war with them. At that time a few German boats and all their crew had been officially taken over by us and they flew our flag.

"Such a boat traveled once in the Mediterranean under German flags, found an Italian steamer, stopped it, saw that it was unarmed and made it show its papers. He saw from the papers that the ship was going to an Italian harbor, and the commander had to let him go.

"Overnight he overtook the steamer and stopped him a second time in the morning, this time under our flag. One of our men was with him, officiating this time as commander, who spoke Italian to the freighter's captain.

"Now it was all right to sink him."

"Why shouldn't we juggle our flags, too? . . . the English have been doing it for a long time."

"But do you know about the situation with the German mine boat? He was supposed to lay mines in front of Malta, but first he wanted to check out the open water through the mine passage.

"As he waited, a mine-searching flotilla came out and set off through the mine passage, looking for enemy mines.

"They had hardly disappeared when he (the German) laid his mines in there, while the Englishman reported that everything was clear.

"As a result, a convoy set out and, sure enough, one of the ships really hit one of those freshly laid eggs.

"The English minesweeper intelligence was immediately relieved of his command because of negligence!"

Now we want to know everything: "How much was sunk in April?"

"Business is booming . . . approximately 900,000 tons."

"And how does it look in the interior?"

"Bad enough to make you sick.

"I was in Vienna a few weeks ago. The *Wazachiten* are going strong.[2] Everywhere they have the final word, wherever you go, in the ministries, with all the authorities, even in the taverns!

The waiters flutter about them. For you, the pig from the Front, there is nothing here . . .

"These damned *"Wazachiten!"*

"Wazachiten? What is that? Is that the lost tribe of Israel?

"You really don't know anything, do you? A *Wazachit* is someone who will make sure he is not going to the Front. They are running around by the thousands, sitting in Central Supply, collecting the money that you gave for iron, but also collecting copper, tin, and all the stuff now being collected, but everyone realizes that they are making business deals.

"Then there are those who take cows out of the farmers' barns and tell them that they should milk the rest longer and more often so that they can deliver more milk.

"Our people stand in long lines from morning until evening so that they can get one eighth of a loaf of bread per person or twelve decagrams of sugar.

"No, no . . . it does not look good at home!" The previously happy mood from telling stories is gone in one blow. Now they all look gloomy as they think the same thoughts.

After a while, I say: "I found here an official letter from the office of the Mayor of Vienna where I am requested to record my name and a motto in the 'Golden Book of Vienna.' Now I know what I will write: 'If you persevere at home, then we will manage on the Front!'"

Everyone agrees.

That was it. That summed it up for all of us.

Twenty-Nine. Otranto

The watch on the Strait of Otranto becomes increasingly tighter. From Italy toward the island of Fanò near Corfu a net is stretched which is supposed to block U-boats from leaving the Adriatic. It reaches deep enough that the U-boats cannot dive beneath it, and the buoy that marks the end of the net constantly shifts eastward. The gap that stays open for the U-boats becomes ever narrower, and north and south of this passage the guard ships hover around, dragging nets in which explosives are installed, and planes scout around over calm seas to find U-boats traveling underwater.

Tethered balloons, which are flown from small steamers, announce from far away the approach of the dreaded U-boats, which are supposed to be forced underwater long before the blockade so that their power and air would give out before they got through the Strait.

In the darkness *U-14* works her way toward the blockade. Much time has been lost by the evasion of a group of destroyers that form the northernmost guard. We have hardly passed this obstacle when we are signaled. Apparently these are enemy recognition signals that demand an answer.

You cannot make out whose signal it is. It comes from the dark part of the horizon and even with the sharp night binoculars, you can't make out anything.

"Dive?" the navigation officer asks.

I hesitate a bit before answering. Diving means loss of time, the night is short—and I must get as far south as possible. One of my fine young officers tries to help out. It is Ilosvay, a Hungarian, a daredevil, who, always cheerful, is ready for any new tricks.

"You know what, sir," I notice from his tone that he has a sudden idea, "if we simply flash back something or other indistinctly, maybe they have enough imagination to read out of it what they're looking for."

"Let's give it a try," I chuckle. And it actually works and we continue unmolested.

The tanks are partially flooded to enable the dive to be as fast as possible, in the event of a surprise.

I suspend even hidden smoking and double the lookouts.

So we continue for another hour.

The man to port has been peering for a while in the same direction. He lifts the night binoculars, rubs his eyes, and looks again. Then he says quietly: "Motorboat!" and then a little later: "I have been watching it for a couple of minutes already."

Hardly distinguishable in the night binoculars, a small dark stripe is traveling on a parallel course at 600 meters.

The watch officer tugs on my sleeve: "There's another to star-board!"

Sure enough, *U-14* is moving in the same direction between two enemy motorboats, as if she belonged to them.

"Dive?"

"Not yet. Let's wait a bit. If they have not yet seen us by this time then they won't recognize us now. Each of them is assuming we are the other one.

"In any case—position the men at the air vents so that everything is ready. We may still have to dive."

The motorboats have torpedo launch apparatus, guns, and depth charges on board. They create a dangerous neighborhood.

But our boat must go as far south as possible before day breaks.

Every nautical mile above water is our gain because by day there is only submerged traveling possible in this region. And planes and tethered balloons can force a U-boat to a depth at which, without the help of a periscope, it would run blindly into the trawler nets.

So we'll press on!

Two at a time the men watch our neighbors and the watch officer stations himself between the two. No one is totally calm in the conning tower. It is a nerve-wracking trip and yet the situation is humorous.

"If they only knew!" young Jlosvay is enjoying the joke, "What they are looking for is traveling between them!"

Below, in the boat the off-duty watch is sleeping and has no inkling. Only the posted watch know they must be ready at a moment's notice.

This goes on for two hours; then the motorboats pull ahead slowly and steadily. The moon has come behind lighter clouds, and as they are moving toward it, they become clearly visible. You could really take them for U-boats!

U-14 stays behind in the dark; after a half hour the escorts disappear.

A couple of wisecracks are sent after them; then it is quiet. No one wants to show how tense his nerves have been.

One after the other the men are sent to the bridge so each can finally have his cigarette.

The engines must deliver what they can. Farther, farther south, the night is nearly over!

Now the journey continues undisturbed. The relief watch comes on deck. With few words we inform him there is "thick air" in the area, and the relieved watch goes below to sleep as soon as the newcomer's eyes are adjusted to the darkness. The customary hot "watch tea" helps dispel any drowsiness.

Only I fall asleep leaning against the guard plate. I have been standing on deck since the beginning of the night.

Gradually it gets lighter. Dawn comes quickly and now the danger of discovery is greatest.

According to dead reckoning the boat has passed the center of the blockade and soon must encounter the southern guard vessels.

"What is that?"

One points forward and already the men tumble into the boat without waiting for a command. They know the custom on board and in twenty seconds the boat is underwater.

First I could not make out what had suddenly appeared in front of the boat. It appears to be a forest of broomsticks as the trawlers' masts suddenly stand there in the half-light. They are traveling slowly westward, and I wanted to try to pass them aft and get around them from behind.

With the increasing light the fishing trawlers become clearly visible. There are twelve of them that search the water in broad formation, and two always drag a net between them.

Soon, soon, we will have free passage again; I breathe a sigh of relief. Then the trawlers turn around and sweep back. Now I cannot pass in front of them; I try to turn completely to starboard in order to get behind them. But before *U-14* is past them, they turn directly toward the boat.

What now? I still try to pass in front of them at full speed. I can use the periscope only infrequently; they are already very close. At the next lookout my boat stands in the middle of their broad front. I cannot dive below them. I could risk a depth of 35 meters, but I have no idea whether or not their nets reach deeper. Staying ahead of them would use up the batteries too much. I have no choice but to go between and through them.

But how?

I must not by any means come between the two steamers that drag a net between them. Once I could see the draglines, I would already be too close; at that point, it would be too late if I were on a head-on course. So I must keep a course parallel to theirs and let them overtake me. If I really come between a net and a dragging pair, I can escape forward at my greatest speed.

Now I must have a look at everything; I must put the periscope out again and again. And the sea is perfectly calm; anyone could easily discover the periscope.

Woe if I am sighted! The steamers are particularly trained and equipped against U-boats.

The steamers constantly change their course; we must make a few turns with them. I have figured out their turning signal.

The sweat is streaming off me. I have already torn off my shirt and jacket; they only annoy me. Scheure, the navigation officer, waits for the command to raise or lower the periscope, whose ocular must be wiped clean because it steams up as soon as I lay my hot eye against it.

Twice the boat ends up between two pairs of ships dragging nets, and I bless my decision to go on a parallel course because I can always come out of it. Once the hawsers are close enough to touch,[1] but the watch on the trawlers' bridges are looking out into the distance, bored, when they could have thrown a grenade on the U-boat's deck by hand . . .

Slowly the last pair passes with its net . . . I breathe deeply and turn toward the south again.

Quickly now the battle helmsman and we officers are handed full mess bowls in the tower. We gulp down the contents hastily.

There is no relief again, for already the next trawler formation is there and blocks the course, constantly weaving back and forth. It's as if we were bewitched! Or are they picking up the sounds of the U-boat?

And so it goes the whole day. We come upon one search flotilla after another.

Toward evening when we have outmaneuvered one last group and can finally surface 3,000 meters from the enemy in order to continue, one of the men says scornfully: "Our moles back home have the sharpest hawk eyes compared to those guys back there!" and points with his thumb toward the trawlers, which keep on searching.

I hope to be able to sleep. For the last twenty-four hours I had been standing uninterruptedly on the bridge and then at the periscope. I am dead tired and so exhausted that I don't want to eat. I must knock off a bit. My three officers and the crew keep watch in three rounds and alternate every two hours.

Shortly after midnight the alarm bell screeches; this calls me to the conning tower. Rudely awakened, it throws me out of my bunk; in a couple of leaps I am there.

"What's up?"

"A destroyer to leeward at two compass-points; he is coming toward us."

"Give me a God's eye."[2] I take the binoculars but see nothing. I have just come out of the boat's bright interior and my eyes must first adjust to the darkness.

"I don't see a thing!"

"But sir, he is almost here; I see him with my naked eye!"

"But where—I don't see anything!"

The destroyer comes roaring at us at 20 knots.

"Sir, if we don't dive, he will ram us!"

"Well, for God's sake, emergency dive!"

There is no question about an attack. Where you cannot see, you can also not fire. After all, the days are gone when you still sank destroyers. The enemy has so many that one more or less makes little difference. Now you must save your torpedoes for the steamers.

A quarter of an hour later, the boat is on the surface again. From now on the "air" is clear.

This time we survived Otranto.

Thirty. Loot

Two days later *U-14* arrives at the hunting grounds that should be the most promising according to the reports of the most recently arrived U-boats.

One steamer route is the course from Cape Passero to Cerigo, the other from Malta to Port Said. The steamships on the first route bring their freight to Salonika for the French army on the Macedonian Front; the others supply the English in the Suez Canal and in Mesopotamia.

This time the first ship out of the convoy that falls prey to *U-14* is a French steamer.

When the sailors from the sunken ship are picked up by a steam yacht and the convoy has continued, we find the site cov-

Fig. 24. A hit steamer

ered with endless wreckage, with many crates and barrels drifting about. What can be in all these things?

Between the chunks of wood something else swims around in circles, and as it comes nearer, it becomes evident that it is an ox. He heads for the U-boat, comes right alongside it, and tries to pull himself up with his forelegs. His hind legs hang weakly down; they seem to be broken. He must be in great pain and feels terribly uncomfortable and helpless in the unfamiliar salt water.

"Look at the poor fellow; he had to go to war, too."

"His backside is totally torn up. It's amazing that he can still swim!"

Fig. 25. A hit steamer

"Sir, this could give us fresh schnitzel!" says one and looks at me longingly. But hauling the badly wounded animal on board would only cause him more pain; I want to spare him that and so the poor animal is put out of his misery.

Now, however, we lift out casks, large and small. The first contains fine French olive oil from Aix, the latter, good red wine.

The oil casks are more important but unfortunately too big. They don't fit through any hatches. I order that the wine be poured out in order to bring the oil on board in smaller casks.

As soon as the torpedo master hears the word "wine," he comes running in order to break the stopper with his own hand. However, he has not exactly understood the command and now stands transfixed as he notices that the good drops are going overboard.

"Don't wait so long . . . get going!" my voice rings out; I watch him surreptitiously and am amused. The torpedo master's face reveals his feelings exactly: at first complete incomprehension—as if he believes he has heard incorrectly—then infinite astonishment; in the end, poorly hidden outrage.

Gurgling, the good red wine flows out of the cask, runs over the deck, and splashes like a small red waterfall into the sea. The torpedo master gazes after it longingly; then he turns around, but I am still standing there. Here comes the oil to be transferred. Disgusted, he turns away and leaves . . . someone else will have to decant it. Men fish out sacks of flour and small barrels of fresh water.

Ilosvay stands on the conning tower and has been observing a spot in the water for a while. He grins, then elbows Scheure: "Watch this!" and points at one of the men who is swimming, chasing after one of the cracked barrels from which candles are pouring. He swims from one candle to another; since he is not wearing a shirt where he can store his booty, he stows them in his left armpit. He has going on twenty candles in his makeshift storehouse; he is full of the joy of the chase and steers with his right hand, farther, from candle to candle. At the same time he does not notice that the candles keep sliding out the back. Finally, he comes on board looking very contented. When he counts his loot, we two officers have to look away so as not to laugh out loud, because he looks so helplessly surprised.

The enemy now constantly devises new means of shaking off U-boats. The newest are the "Allo" messages. For example: "Allo 33 degrees 45 minutes, 15 degrees 31 minutes . . ." signifies a warning to all the convoy, "Pay attention, at this point we have seen an enemy U-boat!" Consequently, the convoy shifts its route approximately twenty miles in order to avoid the U-boats.

Gumpoldsberger, the telegraph master, gives the navigation officer a slip of paper on which is written the latest intercepted telegraph: "Allo 35° 21′, 16° 55′."

He goes to the chart, bends over it for a while, whistles very lightly between his teeth and tells me: "Now they have discovered us!"

As soon as I see the slip of paper with the Allo message, I know what it is about.

"Now, we should know whether the steamers will swerve north or south." At the same time I scrutinize the chart. "You know, let's go that way," and I change course toward the line between Malta and Port Said.

The boat arrives the following morning in her new area and we spot another convoy. This time there are five steamers that come along in two columns. In front, four escort ships provide cover; they cruise, going once faster, then slower, completely erratically. Sometimes they come about and go back—like a small dog whose master goes too slowly. Suddenly they break out to one side in full force, as if they had sighted a U-boat, and occasionally throw small depth charges as scare tactics. They do this adroitly. They had thought this out most cunningly.

Once I comprehend this new tactic I have to smile.

"Really . . . a good joke!" I say appreciatively and in mid-course let the boat slowly sink into the mass of the convoy.

The U-boat travels very slowly in front of the steamers. The sea is moving lightly; therefore the periscope would not be discovered easily. I must use it often; the escorts travel too unpredictably this time.

The most dangerous zone is the destroyers. I must let them pass over me twice. Only then can I pay attention to the steamers.

They are already here and *U-14* slips between the two columns. The periscope lens projects only five centimeters out of the water, so at this eye level the steamers look like giant monsters. The first one comes up at 300 meters now. She lies very deeply in the water, so she must be heavily laden.

Meanwhile Scheure has calculated the firing angle and I let the ship go until the aft stowage compartment is visible through the sight; then I fire a torpedo.

Such a large steamer! And a very sure shot. How many tons?
... But what is this? I had followed the torpedo with my eyes; it
ran straight as a ramrod toward its target, but I hear nothing, no
explosion ... the torpedo must have gone too deep, otherwise I
could not have missed the target!

"Dammit!"

There is just enough time for a curse. By this time the destroyer comes and drops her depth charges; then the last steamer
of the port column breaks away and comes to ram us. It is high
time to dive deep, but you have to keep faith and with the command, "Fire the torpedo!" the boat steers downward to 25 meters and dives under the port column. Depth charges fall behind
us and the destroyer impatiently lets the last steamer pass before
he goes after us.

At the next lookout, the struck steamer has already sunk and
the convoy slowly moves silently on its way. Two fishing trawlers
follow with the survivors.

The crew is looking forward to surfacing—what loot will
there be this time?

But only wreckage indicates the site of the sinking and the
English flag waves over it in the wind. The flagpole is weighed
down underneath and towers perpendicularly in the air. One
man swims over to fetch the flag. The others stand around, disappointed. They had already pictured themselves fishing crates,
kegs, and sacks with very promising contents, but this time there
is nothing. Suddenly one of the men looks out with his hand
above his eyes and stares at a point in the water; immediately
he disappears in the waves. His mates watch him with interest.
What could he have possibly seen?

He swims back with only one hand; in the other arm he holds
something pressed against himself. As soon as he is standing
again on deck, he puts it carefully on the floor—it is a young
kitten. It is dripping wet and looks miserable and meows piti-
fully.

It is accepted lovingly and after a few hours it roams tamely around the men with its fur gleaming. But now it should be christened.

Mitzerl, says her new owner, and looks at her so tenderly that everyone laughs.[1]

"That's nothing to laugh about; every cat is named Mitzerl," he says defensively.

"Not this one, because she is English and only in Vienna are cats called Mitzerl."

"Let's name her Lady; that is English."

"Oh, go on—like the hosiery shop in the Mariahilferstrasse. Actually, now she's been adopted by an Austrian U-boat, so she should get an Austrian name."

"You know what? We will call her Schatzerl!"[2]

Everyone is agreed, and soon Schatzerl is the ship's cat, everyone's favorite.

And no matter how quickly the U-boat has to submerge, Schatzerl is never forgotten and left above.

Traffic in the Mediterranean appears to have intensified, because the next evening a convoy comes out of the West taking a long zigzag course seemingly en route to Port Said.

We get ready for an attack but the steamers come about at exactly the wrong moment and the attack fails.

But in the darkness we overtake the convoy and pick out and sink a large steamer of 8,000 tons.

A large number of crates and sacks swim on the water in the moonlight, but unfortunately they are surrounded by a thick, unappetizing layer of naptha.[3]

U-14 heads for the drifting boats in order to find out the name of the ship. We do not succeed because the letters have been scraped off; instead a pair of blue trousers is in one of the boats. The only loot this time. The owner appears to have been very much in a hurry and they might have impeded his swimming.

One of the U-boat men is delighted with this new addition to his civilian wardrobe.

I take up the pursuit of the convoy and on the following midday we torpedo the next steamer, exactly at the same moment that the leader hoists the signal for the beginning of the general coming about.

This time wonderful things float in the water and *U-14* stops in the middle of the debris field in order to look for the best bits and pieces. Two fishing trawlers return and want to dispute their right to the spoils. They draw near, shooting, but *U-14* defends her valuable loot like a dog his bone and growls at them with her cannon until they turn away again.

Then an almost biblical "catch of fish" begins.

Lard, margarine, oil, flour, sugar . . . nothing but terrific things that we could not find at home now, only in a prewar cookbook.

A chest with the inscription "Fragile" creates a stir and cheerful enthusiasm.

Three men push it in front of them as they swim and bring it on board where it is eagerly anticipated. With a careful heave the chest flies on board.

"What do you think is inside? Maybe eggs?" asks the cook.

"Go on, don't make us laugh at you . . . eggs!" returns another scornfully, feeling superior, "Naturally there's whisky in there!"

"How do you mean . . . naturally?"

"Well, what else would be in a chest off an English freighter with an English inscription and a fragile warning but whisky? You'll see what I mean!"

Soon someone is there with an ax; in an instant the lid flies off and there, clean, in fine shavings, lie neatly placed next to one another . . . lamp chimneys.

With a strong kick accompanied by even stronger language, the chest flies overboard once more.

A boat's compass is taken off one ship; I read the name *Nairn* and look her up: 3,700 tons.

The lucky owner of pants from the previous steamer also finds a jacket here of the same fabric.

I congratulate him about that and promise to do my utmost to shoot a vest out of the convoy so his suit will be complete.

A wallet and a thick bundle of letters are in the blue jacket. Letters from England! Here is direct news from the enemy's homeland—and in recent handwriting.

I get curious. The outcome of so many sunken cargo ships must have finally become noticeable; in England food must have begun to be scarce. You always hear reports of the Central Powers' hopes for the effects of the U-boat war. Now I will corroborate them.

"When someone hungers, he writes about it!" I think and untie a bundle.

The first is a small picture postcard with a poem. Three sisters extol "the heroic sailor who, through storm and bad weather, once at the icy pole, then in the dreadful tropics with their typhoons, masters the sea and far off from his cozy home, sacrifices his life for the fatherland." The cozy home is particularly emphasized. The second card is only signed by Miss Mabel. Then come the letters. At first, news that interests neither the writer nor the addressee, but is what mutual acquaintances will do for the purpose of finding some topic of conversation.

Later the words become warmer, but there is nothing about hunger. Also nothing about butter prices and whether tea has become scarce. Absolutely nothing of interest, only endless sweet nothings. The letters become increasingly ardent and the last ones end with "many kisses from your loving sweetheart Mabel."

Disappointed, I put aside the pack and look through the wallet. There I find the results of a Wassermann blood test: a strong positive.[4]

Poor Mabel, I feel sorry for her.

Thirty-One. Entertainment on Board

The last few days have been strenuous, with attacks day and night, and everyone is pleased that for one whole long, sunny afternoon, the enemy is nowhere to be seen. A day of rest is very welcome.

Complete calm reigns and the sun shines on the iron deck so that the hot air climbs and shimmers over it. The boat lies stopped in the glassy sea, batteries and air bottles are charged and loaded, and the men seek refuge on deck because the heat in the boat is beyond endurance.

Only the sick lie in their bunks. Dysentery has broken out on board and six men lie with high fevers and swallow burned bone powder. The cause, no doubt, is the secret lemonade cupboard that a clever man has installed. He lets compressed air pass through a condensing coil made of copper pipe; the expansion makes it colder. A large water bottle is stuck into this apparatus. The last cargo ship brought lemons. Men come and try to see whether or not they can draw off fresh, cold lemonade.

But the consumption of fresh water increased and the lemonade sale was officially stopped.

On deck we pitch makeshift tents and everyone sits around on blankets and folding chairs. The men are not wearing very much clothing and every now and then one of them jumps into the water. Now and then, for a moment, the engines are started up to give the boat a bit of speed, then the men lie on the half-awash outboard tank and let the water run over them. Later on they will do gymnastics.

On the forward deck a group of men stand with an electrician in their midst. He is worried. He wants so badly to learn the backstroke, but he cannot coordinate it at all.

"Go on, there's nothing to it; just jump in!" one of his buddies encourages him.

"Yes, but my feet always go under, as if they were made of lead!"

At that he gets an idea, and with a mysterious, impish face, he disappears into the boat, to reappear with two life jackets, which are new on board this trip.

"Do you know what? When I tie one of these to each foot, then the feet must stay on top!" and with a clever expression he goes to it.

His buddies are bewildered at this splendid idea. Some are suspicious, others grin apprehensively, but all of them are too curious about how it will turn out to try to dissuade him.

Now the electrician is ready. As he sees only cheerful faces, he looks somewhat suspiciously at his binding.

"Come on now—jump!"

"Come on, get going!" the others urge, and he jumps in.

And then he is gone. Only the pair of black, oily soles of his feet peer out of the water; these kick vigorously; close by, air bubbles come up. The arms are paddling underwater, but they can't bring the head up for air.

Those on deck can't help but laugh. They hold their sides and double up with laughter.

"Someone tickle him!"

Finally it dawns on one of them that he could perhaps swallow too much water. The feet are caught with a boat hook and the back stroker is hauled up on deck.

"Don't you think you should take out a patent for that? It works fine!"

"You rogues, scoundrels, jerks! Wait till I lay my hands on you," he grumbles, still quite breathless.

Then they sit together again.

"What's wrong with the new lieutenant? He's sitting down below and calculating for the longest time," says one man.

"Yes, I gave him a punishment," says Gumpoldsberger quite contentedly.

"But why?" the others want to know.

"Ah—yesterday I got so angry with him and today I counted for him when he shot the sun.[1] So I added a few seconds. Now he's been calculating for two hours already and is making no headway. Let him sweat . . . !"

The ship's lieutenant is sitting below in complete despair. For the fifth time he has calculated the observations and every time the established point falls in the Sahara. I am already impatient and want to know where *U-14* is situated now. How can he tell me, "in the Sahara!"

Then, once again: "Gumpoldsberger, tell the lieutenant, I want to have the chart with the midday position!" I call.

"Yes, sir," but quietly Gumpoldsberger tells his neighbor: "Strobl, you go over; I'll disappear in my quarters."

"Yes, I am coming up immediately," says the lieutenant to Strobl. Then he sees Gunpoldsberger looking out of the door of the radio room.

"You, come over here! Something can't be right. What time did you write down?"

"Lieutenant—according to your 'Stop!'" asserts Gumpoldsberger with his most trusting look.

He didn't even have to lie!

Then he slipped away topside. On his way he meets the first officer.

"Well, Gumpoldsberger, won't you be going on leave when we get home this time?"

"No, sir, I came directly from leave;" but then he has an inspiration. Such an opportune moment will not come again. And already an idea pops into his head.

"But I really need some leave; I must show you something, Sir!"

At once he is back again and brings a photograph that he looks at lovingly.

"Look, Sir, this is Burgl! The daughter of a wealthy manufacturer at home. She's waiting for me. If I came at the right moment, she'd say 'yes.' The last time we couldn't quite agree. It would be good—some leave!"

The first officer looks pleased at the beautiful girl and then says kindly: "She is pretty, really! So go, take your leave. But report back to me what the outcome is!"

"Thank you very much! Yes, sir!" and surprised and happy, he takes off. Would you believe it? He doesn't even know her, most probably she is not even named Burgl; the photograph came into his possession by chance. And now he gets himself a leave. Yes, he must have all the luck!

Then he goes again to his group of friends.

"What did you get out of Pistel again, you old scoundrel?" he is greeted.

"Oh, nothing. He offered me some leave; I did not want to refuse him. Besides, when he sees you with your handsome hat, he will also give you a furlough!" he turns around to another electrician standing near him.

At departure time he had reappeared with a "half top hat" around which he had draped a cap-band with S.M.U. *14* on it.

The next day the black rim in the back was cut off; it had become sort of a cap with visor. The owner removed it when greeting someone with a polite and broad flourish.

On the third day the visor had also been cut off.

Every day that hat became smaller; by now it clung to the back of the electrician's head like a little house-cap.

"You just want it for yourself," he replies to Gumpoldsberger's bantering.

"No thanks, but you can give it to him over there; then he can hold his head up when he wants to swim."

"Are you going to make a fool of me, too?" snaps this one; he grabs the rest of the hat and throws it overboard.

"You jerk! Now you've lost your chance for swimming lessons!"

"Why do I need to learn how to swim? When I come home after the war, I'll marry an innkeeper's daughter; then I'll swim on top!"

"The war will have to be over soon anyway, if we sink all these steamers. But we, too, must be at the parade in Vienna."

ENTERTAINMENT ON BOARD

"Of course, but on horseback; we wouldn't limp on foot."

"You know, I'd recommend a broom; that's safer!"

"Well, you can carry me on your back—they'll think I am one of the camel riders."

• • •

While the men enjoy their "free afternoon," the officers also sit together and smoke. We had just discussed the sick men on board.

"Our men are really good fellows," I say. "Look at how they care for their sick mates and take over their duties. Everything runs so smoothly. It is really a beautiful life we have together on *U-14*!"

"Yes, sir," says one pensively, "and at the same time you must consider that we have on board representatives from every nation that exists in the monarchy. This business with the nationality disputes—I don't believe it. It is only a rumor from a few instigators who want it to happen. Let the men live alongside one another as human beings under a fair command, and look how well it works!" and he points forward to where the men sit together harmoniously and listen to the music of an accordion, which steersman Tefarik plays masterfully.

And it is obvious: it is not only the duties and their responsibilities that force them to get along with one another; no, it is true friendship that binds them together. It is a matter of course for them to accept responsibility for one another.

Thirty-Two. U-Boat Trap

The "Allo" messages about the last two sunken ships lead us to surmise that the steamer route has been shifted again and now *U-14* looks twenty miles farther north.

In the night a convoy comes in sight, this time from the west.

The moon has just set: too light for surface attack and too dark for the periscope.

Fig. 26. The lifeboat of the sunken English steamer *Kilwinning* is visited

We must be patient.

So *U-14* moves ahead of the convoy in order to wait for daylight, and at 5:00 in the morning it is finally time to dive.

There are three ships in front with two submarine chasers of the *Foxglove* type, which, as the story goes, cannot be sunk, even by a torpedo.

A monstrous steamer, heavily laden, travels as right flank man and through a coming about of that ship, *U-14* ends up on the port side. One of the *Foxgloves* steers in a zigzag for a short dis-

Fig. 27. A life raft like those carried by steamers during the war

tance in front of the left transport ship, and it is between these two that I must go to get a shot at the big one.

I must pass directly behind the U-boat hunter so that the steamer that follows does not ram me. The sea is as smooth as a mirror. As I look out at the critical moment, I see directly in front of me the side of a gray ship with a vast porthole; I recoil involuntarily.

"Stop the engines!"

This is tricky! I had all but rammed the enemy by a hair's breadth. Now the submarine chaser travels across my bow and his stern nearly scrapes the conning tower with his depth charges.

Thank God—now he is past!

Then the engines run again and the boat turns back toward the big steamer in order to unload her bow torpedo.

By the next lookout *U-14* is already free of the left steamer. But now we are discovered. I see how the railing of the steamer swarms with soldiers, all intensely gesticulating, pointing to the periscope. The distance is less than 50 meters.

Now the name of the game is to hurry up because naturally the submarine chaser has been alerted!

Right—already he changes his course. But it must have been a false alarm because he turns, going full speed, toward the outside; apparently he presumed the U-boat was out there.

A quick look at the big one. He is just hidden by the middle steamer. When he is free, he will be already so far in front that we can only shoot after him. This will be a difficult shot.

Finally . . . "Torpedo—fire!" and at a sharp angle the torpedo follows the steamer and hits him aft.

Immediately I order a dive to 30 meters. Supposedly the submarine chasers have powerful bombs and we must try to reach a great depth to get as far below the exploding depth charges as possible.

But the depth charges fall far off, and I can soon look out. The hit steamer lies stopped and is lowering his boats, while one of the two *Foxgloves* has come alongside him and seems to be taking on men. Then he moves slowly around the steamer, stops once in a while, and apparently has to work on something in the water.

What the hell is he doing over there? Is he fishing for something? It's odd.

For a long time, he lingers around there and we wonder what he is up to. Suddenly he gathers speed and hurries off after his convoy, disappearing over the horizon.

Meanwhile *U-14* has steered southward and surfaces about 10,000 meters from the steamer. He lies there broad and powerful, in the middle of the Mediterranean, not sinking, not traveling, only enticing: "Come over here, I have so many good things in me that your hungry people could well use! You could get everything free of charge: sugar from India, coffee from the Sunda Islands, tea and silk from China, frozen meat from Australia, and flour and shortening. Think of your hungry families, bring them something! . . . You only need to come and get it!"

He lies there forcefully inviting, offering his goods. All the men are allowed to come on deck to look at the steamer. They so seldom have a chance . . . most of the time they see only smoke and mast-tips and wreckage.

But it is very suspicious to leave a steamer lying there alone. Do they want to wait until the U-boat has left and then tow him? They could not assume that the boat would depart and leave the steamer floating there.

"Was mann nicht erkennen kann Sieht man als verdachtig an,"[1] went a saying around all the U-boats. I remember it just in time.

There is no hurry and *U-14* moves closer. Then a couple of shells fly over there as an experiment. The shots strike on the bridge, on deck, on the stern, at the waterline; everybody strains to see but nothing moves on board.

Again we open fire and the shells shred the smokestack, the superstructure, and the living quarters.

She is a colossal steamer, about 180 meters long. She carries ten huge loading cranes and a number of bulk loading funnels. Something like this seldom travels about.

Slowly *U-14* comes closer. Through the binoculars you can see the damage clearly. But no crewmember is to be seen. Is the ship really deserted?

The sides of bacon beckon on board.

"Let's go over and have a look at the fellow!"

But I am not completely comfortable with this situation.

I am just considering how to board my men onto the steamer because with my three diving rudders on each side, I cannot come alongside in the high swells. Then I see the drifting boats. They give the solution. I only have to take one of the boats in tow and then send the men to board the ship.

I give orders to approach the nearest one, but keep my eye on the steamer through the binoculars. Although everything appears so empty and dead and abandoned, I still have an uneasy feeling.

At the same moment that the U-boat turns away from the steamer, there is the flash of a cannon that had been invisible before. So it was a trap! The first two shots fall short and I am already looking ahead to a gun battle with the poor gunners. But the third shot falls just short of the boat and showers the men on deck with a surge of water. Simultaneously the submarine chaser appears again over the horizon. There can be no more hesitation.

"Emergency dive!"

Cartridge cases are left lying, even a camera, better said, *the* camera of *U-14*—I catch hold of it at the last moment.

"Every man forward and both engines full speed ahead!" The boat submerges, and I breathe a sigh of relief as I see the green water through the side hatches, because during a dive I cannot see the firing.

Another torpedo must be sacrificed.

It is launched at 400 meters directly at the middle of the steamer. Suddenly men appear. Now they see the torpedo coming and scatter forward and aft to avoid the explosion.

But what is the torpedo doing? It runs even slower, then comes to the surface, turns "about face" and sinks.

I cannot spend time wondering about the torpedo's odd behavior because the *Foxglove* is already there. A third torpedo must be readied quickly in order to finally sink the ship.

But now everything has to go very quickly. With the explosion the steamer simply breaks apart in the middle, and after the water geyser collapses and the smoke has dispersed, nothing of the ship is left to be seen.

Our boat reverses course. Suddenly a scraping sound can be heard running from fore to aft along the boat's side. No one can explain it, but it soon stops.

The submarine chaser comes storming toward the sinking site, and while he occupies himself with the rescue, *U-14* has time to disappear slowly northward.

That was our last torpedo, so we must return home. The boat

has been at sea just nine days and she brings home 38,000 sunken tons! That is 3,800 railroad cars at 10 tons apiece! Certainly, the last steamer made up almost one-half of the total.

For the time being, *U-14* must stay underwater because the *Foxglove* is in sight.

We officers stand together at the conning tower. I talk about what was wrong with the torpedo and why it did not hit. It is and remains a puzzle.

"A torpedo can have many defects," I say. "Do you remember the stories of Arnauld de la Perière?[2] He was once torpedoed just outside the Bocche, and the enemy U-boat had fired a whole burst of torpedoes. And the unbelievable happened: one torpedo passed under the boat, the second jumped over it and bent the railing, the third went to the right, the fourth to the left, and a fifth shaved the stern."

"No way! Is that at all possible?" Ilosvay bursts out.

"Arnauld told me himself on his return. I went on board his boat and saw the twisted places.

"A fine man, Arnauld! But that time he was really blessed!"

"But what I wanted to say is that one torpedo can have many flaws—but the way our torpedo behaved could not be attributed to a flaw."

"And why did the submarine chaser first linger so long around the steamer?"

"Yes—and at the end, the scratching outside. Did you hear it, too?"

We ponder over this, and at once everything becomes self-evident: naturally the freighter was left alone there as bait. The *Foxglove* laid a net around the steamer held up by the well-known green glass floats that cannot be seen in a periscope. The camouflaged cannon was there for an approach on the surface; underwater the U-boat would be trapped in the underwater net with her propeller tangled up. The torpedo was caught in these; as long as it could, the torpedo towed the net, but with this weight, it could not reach its goal.

So, a double trap!

"It is pure luck," says Scheure laughing, "that they could not wait to open fire. Otherwise we might have fallen into the trap."

"When we steered toward the drifting boat, they probably thought we had seen through the trick and wanted to leave, so they were in such a hurry to fire."

"Well now, let's have another look," I say.

Through the periscope I see the submarine chaser behind me.

Every ten minutes I check, and after two hours the *Foxglove* is still there. He crosses in long tacks behind the U-boat. He must have defective listening devices because he should have found our boat long ago. Or, maybe it is only by chance that he is looking for us in this direction. It would be all the same, but *U-14* cannot surface as long as the enemy is in sight.

Slowly the battery current runs down. The *Foxglove* does not grow any smaller. The high bridge still shows up over the horizon; she is close enough to find a surfaced U-boat with the naked eye.

But I am getting impatient. This steamship has given me trouble for fifteen hours already! I must surface . . . at the same time I count on poor English eyesight.

Just before surfacing I urge the chief engineer by no means to make any smoke at the start-up of the engines. The cold engines can give off a really awful thick smoke. The boat surfaces and I climb on deck. I immediately regret my decision because at this higher eye level I can see the whole railing of my pursuer. But there's nothing more to do—already one engine has started and dark smoke stinks to high heaven, as if an oil tank had been set afire. The other engine is running, too, and increases the black clouds. We cannot be overlooked!

But the English must have thought the smoke came from a steamer . . . or maybe they did not even see it. At any rate, *U-14* proceeds without harassment.

She could not have made a better smokescreen for herself!

This time the trip through the Strait of Otranto is simple. The boat dives only once because of destroyers; the groups of fishing trawlers can be evaded above water.

En route to the Bocche, the imperial German *U-63* passes us one evening on the opposite course and we shout over to them the observed steamship routes.

In the morning *U-14* lies again in Gjenović.

Thirty-Three. Sheet Lightning[1]

I am sitting in a compartment of the Bosnian train on my way home. The train is overloaded with men on military leave, and whoever did not claim a seat long before the uncertain departure of the train in Castelnuovo must remain standing overnight. But we are going home and such small problems are endured gladly because out of all the cars songs resound:

"Let's go home, let's go home, it is about time . . ."

"In the homeland, in the homeland, we'll see each other again . . ."

" . . . it is about time . . ." Particularly for those who served their four years before 1914 and have worn the Emperor's uniform for seven years.

In the middle of the night the train suddenly stands still. Outside you hear a scream, "Fire!" in German, Hungarian, and Croatian. The sleepy men jump up, everyone grabs his baggage, and in an instant the train cars are empty. Only the U-boat men don't take things so seriously. They have responded to too many alarms to get excited now. First they look out the window and see that only the axles have overheated and that the axle grease is burning. For them the standing is over; they make themselves comfortable on the empty seats, to the great surprise of the others when the train continues.

I have fallen asleep in my corner, but a very young fellow with a fair complexion and red cheeks constantly awakens me. He is restless; he scratches himself, stands up, slaps himself in the face and on the legs and cannot get any rest.

"He has bedbugs," I think to myself and feign sleep because I cannot do a thing to help him. The poor harassed man cannot know that vermin here in the south are considered a sign of health. That supposedly every deloused person avails himself of them again as quickly as possible to insure that he would not get sick!

By and by the exhausted victim falls asleep and his face and hands are dotted with black spots. You think you hear those beasts sucking. After a short time he jumps up again and the dance continues.

I bless the blond man who attracts every bug because that gives me rest from them. In the morning the poor fellow looks unhappy and attacked, but at least he can sleep now because the bed bugs have gone to bed and have crawled away into the upholstery.

Again and again the train must stop along the tracks. It is now autumn and plum season, and Bosnia is the land of the prune plums. For four hours the train travels past fruit trees that are loaded with large blue prune plums. So it is that these involuntary stops, which actually delay the trip, make no one impatient; on the contrary, they are always too short, because some fruit is still hanging after sailors and soldiers have been fetched off the trees.

We finally also survive the second night and reach Bosnia-Brod, the destination of the narrow gauge railway. Here in this rich farmland the farmers still come to market, and I skip a train in order to go shopping. There are things here that can be bought only with great difficulty at home, as they can be obtained only in small amounts from the farmers. It is like paradise! Eggs, butter, lard, onions, cheese, bacon, bread and flour, things the small children born during wartime know only from picture books. I stow my purchases in crates, sacks, and baskets and hope to find porters en route to help me carry all this at the endless railway transfers.

Now I want to continue. There are two possible routes to take home: through Budapest or through Croatia. Through Budapest is by far the more pleasant route. There are not as many changes, and it is faster. So when does the next train to Hungary leave?

"Be so good," I turn around to a young captain who is standing nearby, "and watch my baggage; I will come back immediately."

"You have little time," he answers, "the train is leaving right away!"

"Oh, now, I am going via Budapest, so I still have another hour," as I take out a cigarette and also offer one to the other man.

"I would strongly advise you: do not travel through Hungary! You won't bring a single package through; at the border they will take away everything edible," he answers quickly and urgently.

There isn't time to think it over, hastily to the ticket office and then into the train.

When I finally stow away all my baggage and find a small place to sit, I lapse into heavy brooding. So the Hungarians have cut themselves off . . . what does that mean? They have enough grain, meat, and lard for us all. At home small children are starving . . . and Hungary has placed a blockade.

Now I remember. I had already heard about this in the Bocche; I had just forgotten about it. Because it was so unbelievable, so absurd!

What will come of all this?

During the night I must change in Marburg. There is a couple of hours' layover and I sit down in the restaurant. Cold cigarette smoke and the smell of slivovitz hit me from the big room. All the tables are crowded; most of those present sit on their baggage. The best off are the orderlies. They have made camp on rucksacks and blankets on the floorboards. In any case, they sleep better there than in the trenches.

All kinds of weapons are represented. You can see whether a man comes from the Front or from the homeland. Nothing much is spoken; most of them lean with their elbows on the tables and doze.

A young lieutenant catches my attention. Haggard and pallid, he sits there with a vacant stare. The expression in his eyes is terrifying. The man must have seen and experienced horrible things. His cup of tea, long cold, sits in front of him. He doesn't even see it.

A couple of couriers sit at the next table. At least that's what they look like. They travel in a reserved compartment and seem to be rather important people who come from the A.O.K.[2] They say their wives will come, too. They whisper together and laugh at the latest war jokes.

The lieutenant stands up and sits down farther away.

A train is announced. Many show disappointed faces, others jump up, call their orderlies, gather up their bags, and storm outside. The others sink back into their earlier positions.

Some have awakened completely from the fresh air that came through the open doors, and some write letters. Yesterday they were still with their wives and children after a yearlong separation and tomorrow they will be in the trenches again.

Finally the right train comes and with friendly help I stow the numerous bags in my compartment.

Twice more I must change trains, and then I persuade the engineer with a package of tobacco that my station must absolutely be a stop.

• • •

On the return trip I have the chance to ride from Villach to Laibach on a military train and am marvelously bedded overnight on straw in a freight car. It is the transport of a Hungarian Howitzer battery that is going to the Isonzo Front. Next to me in the straw lie a couple of Hungarian reserve officers. They speak German throughout their conversation.

"What are we doing on the Isonzo Front anyway? We are Hungarians! What does the Italian Front matter to us? We have to defend Hungary, not Austria. How did we get involved in this?"

I think I must have heard incorrectly.

"Did you learn this in Hungary recently?

"Aren't our troops stationed on the Western Front, at Verdun, in Albania, in Syria . . . and you want to defend Hungary only at its borders? Don't you think the Austrian troops also defend Hungary in Galicia and Italy?

"If that is the new attitude in Hungary—then good night."

But the Hungarians show absolutely no understanding of what I mean.

Disgusted, I roll over in the straw. I have become aware of something terribly sad. The old monarchy is visibly crumbling. Who can prevent it? Various Czech units desert, Hungary does not dream only of her independence, but there must be sinister agents who want to sabotage the war. There are rumors of passive resistance in the ammunition factories. In Carniola, in Bosnia, and in Herzegovina, political committees have supposedly been formed.

Fresh air can be found only on the Front and at sea.

Thirty-Four. Bravo, Bim!

I go via Pola intentionally because I have business to do on the flagship *Viribus Unitis*.

I want to look up my old friend, the admiral's aide.

"Hello there, Bim! What's happening here in the fleet? Lots to write about?"

"Terrible!" He throws his hands up in the air and makes a dreary face. "By the way, you are up for another decoration!"

"Aha! That is exactly why I have come here. But not for myself. At this point I have made three trips to the Mediterranean and my men have not even been considered. My boat has not received one award for gallantry. And I am given one decoration after another—I feel embarrassed in front of my men."

"Yes, yes, calm down, it's coming soon; they have all been recommended long ago."

"No, I want to have this now! The U-boats do the dirtiest work and honestly deserve their medals. The men are beginning to try to transfer to the air corps because over there they are treated better."

"But it's coming! I tell you—the dispatch must already be underway!"

"Good! Then I will go and wait until the decorations arrive. Until then, I will not put out to sea. So hurry up! By the way, we remain friends."

I have the chance to travel on a steamer to the Bocche. During the day the route goes between the islands because here fewer enemy boats are expected. The stretches toward the open sea are navigated overnight. Even here the darkness is perceived as protection from U-boats!

In the course of time the enemy has already sunk a few steamers on this stretch. Once even a hospital ship. But this life-giving transport for fleet and army was never interrupted along the home coast all the way to Durazzo. There the Austro-Hungarian fleet held naval supremacy. To the end!

For me as a U-boat man this steamer trip is of great interest. I see the other side of economic warfare and help diligently to look out for periscopes.

When I arrive at Gjenović, I find my boat all ready to sail; but I find something else and am frankly astonished: a telegram that announces decorations for my men.

Bim is a fine fellow, on whom you can depend! So prompt— bravo!

"Tonight we put out to sea!"

Thirty-Five. **Autumn Journey**

In the Strait of Otranto *U-14* must submerge in front of a group of fishing trawlers and continue submerged aft of them. Slowly the vessels move away and, after a short while, our boat surfaces again.

Then the rudder gets stuck. At ten points to port the boat travels in circles.

The manual rudder is engaged, useless; the failure must be in the steering transmission in the boat's interior or else outside.

Now we investigate. The men tear off the coverings of the transmission shafts with greatest speed. In the narrow space aft—which is crammed full with pipes, magnetic compass, propeller shafts, and air pumps—the men work in the most impossible body positions. In order to expose the entire transmission, a couple of pipes must be dismantled.

The fishing trawlers come about, return, and we cannot move from the spot. There is no way for us to evade the trawlers! The defect had better not be outboard! Only a diver can repair that, and there are none on board.

I stand on the bridge. One look at the fishing trawlers, then I call below: "You still haven't found anything? We have to get out of here soon!"

The torpedo master's head, red as a tomato, uncoils from the entanglement.

"Not yet, sir, but I will have it soon."

The transmission shaft is exposed to the aft diving tank. Now they can only check there. If the failure is not discovered there, it lies outside, and we are lost.

The manhole of the aft diving tank is tightly shut with many screws and now must be dismantled. The men work feverishly. Something in my voice pushes them to work their fastest, but it does take time until the many screws are unfastened.

The fishing trawlers move ever closer.

Fig. 28. *From left to right:* Ilosvay, von Scheure, von Trapp, Pistel

Now the torpedo master steps into the tank. At this point diving is impossible.

There—

"A hammer and a wrench!"

The requested tools are handed to the torpedo master.

"What did you find?"

"A broken and jammed crosspiece," then he hammers and finally the parts of the connecting piece come off.

The trawlers are approaching awfully fast, but I do not mean to make the men nervous, and I keep the imminent danger to myself. Only the gun is readied inconspicuously.

The crosspiece must be exchanged but there is no spare on hand. Finally the same connecting piece is found in another place, where it can be spared for the time being. It is quickly dismantled.

At any moment the boat can be seen.

"Son of a gun, how much longer will it take . . . ?"

And simultaneously the reply, "All clear!"

Fig. 29. Rest day on board S.M.U. *14* in the Mediterranean

At full speed *U-14* manages to pass the broad front of the search flotilla . . .

• • •

It is now fall and the Mediterranean is no longer the same.

Cold winds from the north and moist winds from the south alternate constantly and herald winter. It is not swimming weather any more. When it is calm, a misty horizon blocks the view and the U-boats' prospects become scanty.

The first convoy comes, this time out of a rainsquall. There are four steamers accompanied by a *Foxglove*, a destroyer, and three fishing trawlers.

U-14 counts on the rain this time. There can be no sharp lookout, and the periscope cannot be seen as easily, so the U-boat can approach from outside the group and catch a steamer.

Immediately the depth charges come. This time they are so strong and powerful that a fuel tank springs a leak outside and in. So *U-14* must let the remaining three steamers get away and await the sinking of the ship from a great distance in order not to betray herself to the U-boat destroyer by her oil leak. I see from far away how this one circles the sinking steamer at high speed, while the fishing trawler picks up the steamer's crew. Finally both take their course in the direction of their convoy and are shortly lost in a wall of rain.

Toward evening perfect calm sets in. From the crossed swells it is evident that the southeast is fighting with the northwest, and where they meet—we know this already—there are sparks. Sure enough, there is sheet lightning in the south, and a thunderstorm approaches. Very quickly it gets dark, the heavy clouds are dark as night, and after a short while, you cannot see your hand before your eyes. Only the sheet lightning becomes more frequent, sending its blinding bursts of light into the heavy mass of darkness. There is no thunder yet; it is as if Nature is holding her breath waiting for what is still to come.

"Stop the engine!" There is no point in trying to keep a lookout now.

The men stand in groups on deck; the heavy stillness is burdening them as well. No one talks; everyone stares spellbound into the dark night that encircles us, frequently torn apart by dazzling lightning and pulsing swaths of light leaping up.

Then, almost swallowed up by crashing thunder, we hear a

shout from the bow. A brilliant white lightning flash snatches away the protective darkness for a split second, and I see a small convoy quietly passing a few miles away.

Now the storm has burst on us, the spell has broken. Both motors full force ahead. "Torpedo one, three, seven ready! Is your cat below?" resounds through the night. *U-14* takes up the chase.

The U-boat heaves to at first, ascertains the general course of the freighters, and then sets out for the dark weather-side. We must attack from the surface.

Now where is this light coming from? A moment ago it was pitch dark! Suddenly it is evident that marine phosphorescence has set in, as intense as is normally seen only in the tropics. The bow wake makes so much light that you could read, and a luminous streak accompanies the boat.

An attack by marine phosphorescence is something new, even for me. Our boat must be conspicuous for many miles around. We will be discovered for sure. Straining, I look to see whether I can observe such illumination also near the enemy. But there everything stays dark and only the incessant lightning keeps us from losing sight of him.

But how does it look underwater? How deep does this marine phosphorescence extend? Could it be possible for the boat to drag a silver streak behind her in 15 meters' depth and betray herself with it? A splendid target for the expected depth charges!

I promise myself to investigate this later, during more peaceful times.

Meanwhile, the tanks are flooded in order to dive immediately if necessary. Through the diving rudder, the boat maintains a steady, fast speed above water.

Suddenly the steamers turn more toward the boat, and in order not to come too close, we must reduce speed.

I stand alone on the conning tower, focusing all my attention on the shifting target in the periscope. At the same time I am unaware that the U-boat is slowly sinking below me.

The whole deck is already awash; now the water climbs higher on the conning tower until it runs over my feet—only then I notice it and I have just enough time to close the hatch.

What is going on? I am literally losing my footing. I pull myself over to the railing, and climb from there farther up on the struts of the net catcher.

I understand perfectly how it happened: due to the decreasing speed the boat's diving rudder could not keep the heavy boat on the surface anymore and so it is slowly sinking.

I know that my second-in-command will raise the boat before it sinks from under me. I have only one concern: that the moment of attack will slip by. I have no method of communication with those in the boat. I cannot respond to any enemy movement. Meanwhile, the boat sinks farther; my last hold is the raised periscope.

Then, finally the boat rises with increasing speed; I have just enough time to tear open the hatch and to call below my orders to fire.

The steamer must have been loaded with ammunition because the explosion is violent and there is a gruesome picture of bursts of fire and a shower of sparks falling down, lighting up the entire convoy.

Then everything is dark again. With one last long reverberating thunder roll, the storm has spent itself, and the convoy disappears in an oncoming rainsquall.

For several days the weather cannot seem to make up its mind. Between the two competing winds, one storm after another breaks over us, and heavy rainsqualls make the U-boat men take out their winter gear. Now it is comfortable in the boat's cabin, and we are reluctant to leave the warmth coming from the engines. Also, all the clothes are wet and there is no way to dry them. So it is always best to do what I do.

"That wet stuff is just like a hot compress!" I grumble, pulling off wet clothes and lying down in the buff. Then I immediately fall asleep.

Suddenly the alarm screeches above my head. This is used only when it is extremely urgent. Abruptly torn out of my sleep, I jump to the conning tower, just as I am.

In the twilight a convoy comes into view not far astern. It is high time to submerge. Teeth chattering, I stand on the tower; I want to get my bearings first before the boat dives. In my bunk it was warm, but here an icy wind is blowing—and I am shivering.

I want to look through the binoculars, but I can't; I am shaking too badly. Then pants, a sweater, and shoes are handed up from below, and while I hurriedly dress myself, the watch officer describes the situation to me. By then we already see the ships with the naked eye.

Two *Foxgloves*, which cruise ahead of four steamships, do not permit a long observation, and ten minutes after the alarm screeched, the boat is underwater, and the torpedoes are ready. *U-14* steers toward the convoy from the side. We pass in front of a column; there is just enough time to turn in between the two lines, when a *Foxglove* turns directly toward our boat.

I do not know: Is this a random turn or have we been discovered? In the second case, we must go to the greatest depth immediately to reduce the shock of the depth charges. But then we will lose the chance to attack. So I continue and let the submarine chaser approach me.

The sea is quite rough, the freshening wind whips up whitecaps and the danger of being discovered because of the periscope is not great. The enemy comes rushing on at full speed; *U-14* needs to decrease her speed. The *Foxglove* crosses her course right in front of our bow. Threatening, the dreaded depth charges hang onto the broad stern, and a man stands nearby, ready to let them drop.

"If he only knew!" goes through my head, but it is 5:00 in the morning, and before breakfast, the man's thoughts presumably focus on the kitchen.

By this time *U-14* is right in the middle of the steamers.

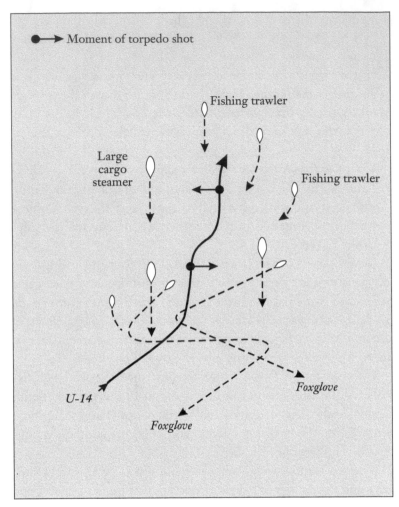

Fig. 30. Illustration of an attack on a convoy by *U-14*

"Torpedo three—fire!"

But to starboard the torpedo fails. The last depth charges must have dented some of the torpedoes again! I turn to attack the second steamship from the bow, but a third steamer is already there and threatens to run over me. I must turn back quickly in order to be able to fire to port.

There is no more time to watch; here come the depth charges . . .

As we descend we hear the first direct hit, then depth charges follow of such power that our whole boat rocks up and down.

Soon after, I see the usual picture in the periscope. The heavily laden ship lies with her bow deep in the water. Fishing trawlers take on the crew and after two hours, the steamer goes perpendicularly into the deep. A drifting raft is all that remains of her.

Thirty-Six. Internal Duty

The northwester had blown itself out. At first it brought more heavy rainsqualls, but then the sky lightened and the wind increased to force 8. An attack is impossible in the heavy seas. Two hospital ships steam by to the north; our boat evades them and then, with one engine running slowly, holds her course into the sea. U-14 swims on the water like a duck. The boat is constantly awash, the only halfway dry place is provided by the conning tower. So the off watch men are crowded into that space to snatch some fresh air.

Down in the boat it is terrible now. The hatch must be half closed against the oncoming sea and, except for one machinist's mate, who is called the "iron reserve" because "it" never "catches up" with him, nearly everyone is seasick. Coming from the tower out of the fresh salty sea air into the boat's interior takes away your breath. Hot fumes rise up to meet you—a sickening mixture of oil, cooking odors, and sweat stench. Immediately each man heaves and only a rapid flight back to the tower can help. But it is the changing of the watch; you must go below. In addition, that continuous lurching and pitching—only the most robust stomach can stand that.

The watch officer turns to the radioman, whose collateral is supply petty officer.

"Gumpoldsberger, what's being cooked today?"

"Sir, today we are making schnitzel; we have a great number of them preserved!"

"Very good, let's go! It will soon be midday. By the way, which stations have you picked up today?"

"None, sir. I have not been able to pick up any. The antenna is constantly awash."

Then he disappears—sighing—in the boat and wants to fetch the cook. He finds him lying in his bunk, pale and retching.

"Cook, let's go! You need to cook now!"

"But sir, I feel sick!"

"Not sick! Puke, and then let's go!"

Back in the harbor, schnitzel had been put up carefully in glass jars.[1] They are stowed away in the provisions cabinet. Gumpoldsberger opens the door and recoils. A revolting stench streams at him. With averted head he reaches in and pulls out a jar. The lid is removed and the meat is rotten. It stinks dreadfully. The second glass jar looks exactly the same.

"Such a rotten mess! Cook, come here! Now take the jars out—but do not throw up!"

The cook does not comprehend the situation, sticks his head in, and wants to look. But only for a second; then he bursts out with his hands covering his mouth and runs to the nearest head.[2]

"You pig!" is all that the petty officer can muster up in sympathy; then he works on, holding his nose. One jar after the other stands there facing him, completely spoiled, and he must get help to empty them overboard. At one time subatmospheric pressure must have existed in the boat, which loosened the jar lids. The clouds of stench are not so easy to dispel; everyone complains loudly about this awful mess, and it isn't even the radioman's fault.

For lunch instead of schnitzel there is only bread and cheese, and the radioman gets sidelong glances from the crew.

Then I send for him: "Where is tonight's war report?"

"I have not had any reception, whether from Pola, Nauen, Osmaniye, or Malta."

"OK. But tonight you try a little harder. For two days now I have had no news!"

"Yes, sir."

By the next morning the wind from the northwest has risen to force 10 and the seas have increased. The ingenious cook has produced tea served with ship's biscuits. At noon, cold tinned food; in the evening, bread and cheese again.

"Say, Gumpoldsberger, if you don't give us anything else to eat, you could at least supply me with the war reports!"

With a despairing face the radioman disappears in his magic booth.

For an hour he sits there, but he is not able to pick up any signals.

The whole boat is already mad at him, the officers and I grumble, his comrades threaten to beat him up, and the cook cannot leave his bucket. His last hope is Nauen, which should send the war report at midnight. He searches for it again and again, trying to hear something. But there is simply nothing.

Without a moment's hesitation, he sits down and resolutely writes: "Western field of operations: At Paschendaele, in a surprise attack, our gallant troops have taken a section of army trenches and taken captive 200 Frenchmen and 300 Englishmen. In the eastern section of Chemin-des-Dames, the French set after strong artillery preparation, attacked our position and were repelled bloodily. Northeast from Soissons our troops are withdrawn in the prepared positions.

"On the southwest front there is nothing new . . . etc."

"Perhaps the old fellow will be satisfied now!" he murmurs and brings me his war communiqué.

"Well, bravo!" I praise him, read the fraud with interest, and am appeased.

The following morning the northwester continues to blow with unbroken velocity, the gyroscopic compass is useless, and the boat continues on by magnetic compass.

In the morning Gumpoldsberger hauls out the cook, places him before his cook stove in the forward torpedo space, and helps him open the cans of food: goulash, and Leipzig stew.

Everything is to be mixed and then heated.

The boat rolls firmly, farther. The cook has the big pot between his knees and stirs. Gumpoldsberger stands next to him and watches. A heavy sea comes, lifts the bow and with it also the cook . . . he bends far over and thank God everything lands outside the far side of the pot. Gumpoldsberger spurs him on: "*Cogo*, hurry up, or you'll puke into the pot!"[3]

The sweet smell of the goulash rises in the cook's nose so much that he retches, again it comes but this time so quickly that half of it goes into the soup.

"You pig!" Gumpoldsberger chokes out. In his mind he can picture the threatened thrashing. He looks around discreetly. His comrades are lying in their bunks sound asleep. No one has seen anything, so he turns back to the wholly contrite cook: "Keep on stirring, you pig!"

Later at lunch, officers and crew praise him for the delicious Leipzig stew.

Thirty-Seven. Intermezzo

U-14 is getting a new battery and travels via the Dalmatian islands toward Pola.

Then a motorboat comes toward her and brings the order to moor at Olive Island near the docks. At 8:00 in the morning Emperor William will come on board![1]

One hour is still enough time to straighten up the boat, to wipe away the traces of the Mediterranean trip, and to dress up for the reception. A wide gangway is placed on board, and on land, gathered expectantly in front of the boat, stand those ordered to the reception.

The Emperor appears punctually, briefly greets those present, motions away every attendant, and comes on board alone, where I give him my report.

His first movement is toward the cannon, and he asks some questions about it and about the successes of *U-14*.

Then he inspects the crew, which is lined up aft starboard.

"Which nationalities do you have on board?"

"Your Majesty, nearly all that there are in the monarchy: Germans, Hungarians, Italians, Romanians, Slavs, Poles . . . but on U-boats everyone must be able to speak German."

"Do you see how important the German service language would be in Austria!"

I am at a loss for an answer.

Thirty-Eight. In the East

In Romania a small Russian U-boat is captured on the Danube and I receive an order to evaluate whether it could be used in the Adriatic. I am to travel to Bucharest to inspect it.

They know nothing there. I am sent on. I should get information in Braila near the Danube monitors.

So I travel the twelve hours to Braila.

There I discover that the boat has been brought to the shipyard at Turn-Severin; I should go there.

I find a steamer that brings me back on the Danube through all of Romania in two days, and finally find the U-boat.

It is much too small and quite neglected. It could not be used in the Adriatic; at best it could give tours on one of the Upper Austrian lakes.

It was supposed to have operated in the Danube against her monitors; after the Russian armistice, it was hidden by her crew between steamers and tugboats and then abandoned.[1]

In Romania the position of the monarchy is judged pessimistically. Here, in proximity to Hungary, Russia, and the south Slav lands, you hear many things that you dare not think about in Vienna and near the Adriatic. The possible abdication of the monarchy is spoken of openly, also of "Emperor Karl, the last." These questions are not considered problems, no, only as something unavoidable.

I am indignant. Such discussion among officers! I want to snap in reply, to refuse to tolerate that kind of talk.

Fig. 31. A "harmless" steamer, but the U-boat's downfall

"My dear friend, that's the way it is; we cannot do anything about it! Why play the hiding game? You must also have the courage to face the facts of the matter. We are finished! We could have known that for a year already, had we removed our blinders. We simply did not want to see. Our Emperor has already tried, but we can no longer get peace. Germany still insists on "peace through victory."

Wherever you look mistakes have been made, and they are still being made.

From the peace with Russia we anticipated food from the Ukraine. Yes, *Schmarrn!*[2] The little bit that came to Austria did not go far.

In the forests of Slavonia the "green guards" prowl about, deserters from all lands of the monarchy. You would have to send an army over to capture them. The rural police don't dare to take action against them anymore; they are too strong. Whenever things aren't going well, he just joins the troops; it is a strange coming and going over there.

Fig. 32. The trip home toward Pola

Carniola, Bosnia, and Herzegovina are already breaking away. Look at the newspapers: the most beautiful real estate in Carniola is dirt cheap. Anybody German is fleeing toward German lands.

Everything is falling apart.

Now they hold meetings in Vienna, one after another; they want to make amends for what for years has been neglected. But what they could have granted earlier is now demanded—and God knows what more. They could have relied on gratitude previously, now only disdainful laughter.

But what am I saying? We must expect that those "above" know what is to be done. We will be the ones to take the consequences.

Besides, tomorrow a Hungarian steamship leaves for Ada-Kalé. A pleasure trip. Come along! All the officers are invited. It's going through the Iron Gate; you could look at that, for once.[3]

Totally disheartened, I turn away and cannot sleep for a long time.

Ada-Kalé is a Turkish island in the Danube. It was forgotten by one of the peace treaties and remained Turkish. The people make their living from smuggling. Here you can get Turkish cigarettes!

In the morning I am on the pleasure cruiser. It is swarming with guests, chiefly German officers. Everyone is invited by the steamship line. On the foredeck the captain pours out shots of cognac. It is a hundred years old. At least he says so. In the dining hall the tables are loaded. It is like life was before 1914, delicacies already long forgotten. Pasties, roasts, bacon, caviar, wine, beer, schnapps. It is never ending. Salt sprinkled breadsticks and croissants are replaced by the basketful.

In Austria the little children don't even know what white bread is; they eat turnips.

Thirty-Nine. The Fire Goes Out

In Fiume large U-boats are under construction. Two at 700 and two at 500 tons. The commander of *U-4* and I are to get the two larger boats, and, until their completion, I take over the command of the U-boat station in the Gulf of Cattaro.

The number of U-boats has grown. The new ones work in the Mediterranean; the old ones stay in the Adriatic.

In Gjenović a small arsenal has been built with workshops and warehouses for spare equipment, and the management prides itself on accomplishing all repairs on location. Only major repairs must be undertaken in Pola.

Also, the barracks do not suffice for quarters any more and S.M.S. *Monarch*, the old coastal defense ship, becomes the residence ship moored at the station.

Bombproof shelters are under construction and Russian prisoners of war are assigned as handymen. The hospital is enlarged and a newly laid out vegetable garden supplies the sick and the healthy. Pigs and hens are being raised.

To ensure that all these culinary products will be correctly utilized, a cook is hired. One officer who is going on leave brings her from Graz, the city that, since time immemorial, has produced cooks for the navy. A wonderful older woman who soon becomes accustomed to her new surroundings and puts all our troubled stomachs in order.

There is only one thing she cannot get accustomed to, and that is the air raids. They are terribly painful for her. She is not very mobile and cannot run very far. Every time the sirens scream and everyone hides for safety in the bombproof shelters, she hurries under a small, flimsy bridge that leads over a dried-up streambed. She believes herself safe there.

Besides—these planes! Normally they appear daily at 7:00 in the morning. Their target is the U-boat station. But until now they have not caused any damage. The defense works too well and most of the bombs fall into the water and explode there. Every time, the motorboats and tenders race to the explosion site in order to catch the fish with hand nets and the most incredible scooping utensils, as the fish lie stunned on the surface. You must hurry up because in a short while, they come to and swim away.

Although the planes have not caused any serious problem up to now, they can still annoy. The U-boats must leave their moorings and submerge for the duration of the attack, which greatly delays the work. Also, the men must abandon the workplaces to go to safety under the armored deck of the *Monarch*.

Like all seamen, I am superstitious. I would never leave port on a Friday! And it is absolutely impossible for me to ever put on the right shoe first. That would bring horribly bad luck!

Once again the air raid signal sounds, as usual, early in the morning. I jump out of bed and dress quickly. The orderly is just polishing my shoes and comes running with one shoe that is polished. It is the right one! By now bombs are exploding all around—but to put on the right one first would mean certain destruction. So I wait for my left shoe and then everything else goes according to plan—nothing happens.

Contented, I go to my daily work. As so often before, the left shoe has prevented trouble. Well now, how easily a bomb could have hit me today!

• • •

This is the Austrian U-boat station. The German station lies a couple of miles farther toward the interior of the Gulf. There is a beautiful, amicable relationship between the allied colleagues, and frequent get-togethers promote further cooperation.

Today we are giving a feast. A "Jarac"—a sheep, also called "Dalmatian coastal deer"—roasted on a spit, is something unknown to the Germans, and they should have a taste of this delicacy. Sheep are not scarce in the Bocche even in wartime, and way ahead of time three local sailors receive orders to prepare the banquet.

They are specialists in their field. On the slope behind the U-boat station under olive and fig trees, a slow-burning fire is prepared of stone oak branches, and above the embers and the slowly burning wood three sheep roast on their spits, which are continually turned slowly to roast all sides evenly. Secret herbs are used to make the roasts savory.

The task suits the three sailors. Taking turns, one is always turning the spits, the other two lie on the grass on their backs, staring at the sky or sleeping, arms crossed under their heads. It is the most peaceful picture.

Into this idyllic scene, shrill sirens wail from all the ships: air raid. Totally off schedule, the planes have come in midday. According to orders, "everyone" must go under cover, and in great leaps the aroused hurry downward.

There everyone crowds on the floating dock toward the S.M.S. *Monarch* and Kršnjavi, the commander of *U-40*, has trouble pushing against the flood of the station's personnel as they stream aboard.

"Where are you going?" someone asks him.

"My sheep! They will be stolen!" and he works his way through the crowd.

Then he races uphill, finds the mutton still safe, and flings himself down near them exhausted, while all around him bombs are flying. He was given charge of the feast and he feels responsible for it.

He doesn't even think about the air raids.

Then the enemy planes disappear toward the sea, pursued by our own planes. The station motorboats again fetch their fish. The roasting continues.

It is shortly before sundown and the time for the evening flag salute, the lowering of flags on all ships and vessels.

Through the peaceful, calm evening, the bugle calls resound

to the mountains above, calling those on watch on the guns to give the flag its honor salute. Two men stand bareheaded on deck, ready to lower the war flag. All around, solemn silence prevails and those Austrian and German officers by the fire can watch the sunset over the Prevlaka peninsula. The sun sets like a dark red ball diving into the water, becoming ever smaller, and then the top rim disappears.

Then the cannon resounds from the admiral's ship.

The flag salute.

The mountains echo it, and slowly and solemnly the melody of the old Imperial anthem, the *"Gott erhalte,"*[1] resounds while the venerable imperial flag, crowned with glory, is taken down. Everyone stands saluting with his gaze fixed on the image, until the last note fades away.

Our allies lie in the harbor, the German U-boats, and in the same solemn manner the German national anthem is saluted. With the prayerful refrain, "Father, I call unto you!" the ceremony ends and the buglers sound off gaily on all the ships.

The fires have burned down to embers; the man at each spit looks as if he would be more comfortable in his native costume, the wide Bosnian pants, the shirt, and the open vest and little red cap. The spits are turned slowly and the fat drips onto the embers. It would be customary, no doubt, to sit around the fire, to slice off a piece of the roast, to pass the wine jug, and sing old Slavic melodies. But Kršnjavi, who organized the festivities, had made things elegant and set tables under the olive trees.

The heavy Dalmatian wine soon loosens the tongues and someone begins to sing the "Ballad of the *Emden*." Someone from the North has brought it here. It follows an old sailors' melody and describes the sinking of steamers, the joys that the pirated freight on the *Emden* creates, and the saddened remarks of the captured captains.

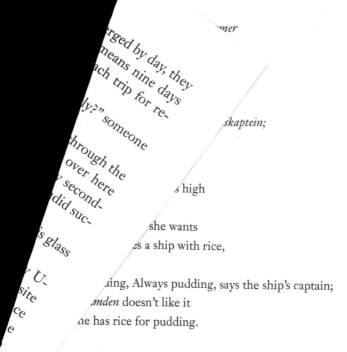

mer

rged by day, they
means nine days
ach trip for re-
ly?" someone
hrough the
over here
second-
did suc-
s glass
U-
site
ce
e

skaptein;

s high

she wants
s a ship with rice,

...ing, Always pudding, says the ship's captain;
mden doesn't like it
...e has rice for pudding.

...a sugar ship comes, then a ship with cinnamon, just in ...r the rice pudding, and the next ones bring coal and rum. ...e last verse the *Emden* is sunk, the pirating ends, but a new *nden* will arise and carry on the tradition of the first one.

Despite all the good intentions, the mood doesn't seem right. The Bulgarian front is shaky, nothing is certain, but the K.u.K. U-boats are not allowed into the Mediterranean any more. They are to protect the Montenegrin and Albanian coasts. Leaves to Bohemia are discontinued, why, no one knows; then it is reported that Hungary has called back her troops.

An oppressive atmosphere prevails. No one knows what's what, but no one will complain. The German officers are better informed, but they say nothing.

On the ships, discipline is not the same. The men want to go home.

The U-boats continue to work; they are in good form, as never before. The weather-tanned faces have become pale. Each

ime they go out they stay for nine days; subm
surface at night to charge the batteries. That
without sun. They are given three days after e
pairs, then they go out to sea again . . .

"Hasn't Seyffertitz sunk a French U-boat recent
asks me.

"Yes that's true; let's ask him about it!" And I look
ranks and call over to a nearby table: "Hugo, come
and tell us about your *Circé*!" Seyffertitz had been m
in-command on *U-5*, and I am truly pleased at his sple
cess.

Seyffertitz, the commander of *U-47*, comes over with h
of wine and joins us.

"Three weeks earlier, by Cape Pali, I rammed an enem
boat, and—isn't it funny—I met the *Circé* at exactly the same
at night. But at the first approach I underestimated the distar
and my torpedo never made it to its target. When I surfaced, I
was gone. But I knew his course and chased him. After half an
hour I caught up with him and then placed myself in front, always parallel with him, with him always in the moonlight. After
three hours I had another chance to fire.

"But just imagine my shock: as I arrived at the location of the
sinking, someone cried out of the water: *Hilfe!*[2]

"Can you believe it? In German. I thought I had sunk one of
our boats," he turns to us. "Two of my men jumped into the water and hauled him out. When I learned that he was French I was
relieved. If he hadn't been I would never have forgiven myself.
He thought I was an Englishman. On the other side they had
sunk each other several times.

"We had rescued the *Circé*'s watch officer. He had neither
heard nor noticed his boat's sinking. He just suddenly found
himself in the water. He looked like a student after a duel and
got his share of teasing after that.

"Right then his wife was on her way from Paris to Brindisi to
meet him the next day. And so that she would not get frightened,

the radio station in Castelnouvo broadcast in clear language that he was the only one of the *Circé* crew who was rescued. So she was able to read this upon arrival in Brindisi in a special edition of the newspaper.

"By the way—he was called Lapéreyre. Almost like Arnauld.[3] Where is Arnauld now?"

"He's commanding a U-cruiser and might be in the Atlantic. Do you know how much he has sunk so far? About 400,000 tons!"

"Yes, yes, he is a terrific fellow . . . God, please let our U-boat war succeed! At home it looks terrible!"

"Last week I spoke with my brother in Vienna," another interrupts, "he is stationed on the Isonzo Front. It is much worse than we can imagine! It is really a miracle that our men are still fighting. They have no uniforms anymore, and only every third man has a coat. They are running out of ammunition, and food is getting scarce, too. They are fed black coffee and dried vegetables and occasionally, when there is plenty, they get a small piece of cheese. Their underclothes are in tatters. When they finally come to wash, they must wait until their old rags are dry because they don't have anything to change into. It is awful."

And then news comes from home: everything is being confiscated from the farms. The last droplets of milk, every egg is taken away. There is hardly any compensation for it. It wouldn't be so bad if the food would benefit at least the hungry population! But everyone knows that all the requisitioned food will be sold again on the black market at exorbitant prices.

"In such a situation, I, too, would hide butter and eggs!"

"These crooks, the war profiteers and black marketers, they get rich and stuff themselves full. The burden is on the backs of our soldiers, farmers, and the respectable people who honor their ration cards.

"Tell me, can we wage war that way much longer?"

"The current officials are being shoved out. Headquarters is

filled to the brim with newcomers who have an uncle or someone like that who is 'indispensable.' It is an awful mess!

"And this is supposed to be the 'grand time?' We should erect
gallows and hang these corrupt war profiteers. Just wait, when
the war is over they will be on top, acting like 'big shots!'"

Slowly the discussion subsides.

No one dares say it aloud: and what happens when our fronts
collapse . . . if we have to surrender . . . ?

We mustn't even think about that!

As the discussion breaks up, everyone is full of confidence
again. We will not give up. Three boats are ready once more
and the next morning they will put out to sea.

Happily they go down together, but two of us stay behind.
The fire is completely burned down and we spread out the embers.

"Do you know why the fire has gone out?" I ask.

The other one looks at me surprised.

"Because no one put wood on it . . ."

If our men endured at the Front, it is thanks to their untiring
loyalty, the passed-on tradition. Without this spirit in the army
they would have dispersed long ago. In that condition! The enemy work systematically in the interior to wear down our own
Front, and our men fight like heroes.[4]

"Our people are a marvel . . ." I start again.

"What are you going to do after the war?"

"Continue to serve—naturally! The work will start only now;
we will have to rebuild anew. Now, after so many war experi-
ences, things will have to change!"

"Yes, but what if . . ."

"What—when?"

"Go on, come on board with me. I still have some slivovitz,"
he urges me.

"Yes, I'd love to; I can't sleep anyway. But what do you mean
by your 'if'? You are behaving strangely tonight!"

He says urgently, "Did you see the maps that show how the

Allies propose to divide Europe? And did you notice what would be left of Austria? One small dot. Without a coast!"

"My God, has it already come to that?"

"Well, what will you do then?" he asks.

"I don't know. Where do I belong actually? Where am I really at home? Nowhere at all! Father: navy officer. I have absolutely no relatives in Austria . . . it's in the navy that I am at home, or, if you will, at sea!

"And what about you?"

He responds, "I, too, am an officer's son. Born in Galicia, elementary school first in Bohemia, then in Sarajevo. We were pushed around the entire monarchy. My father is on the Isonzo Front, my mother lives in Vienna."

"Yes—where am I at home?"

"Well, there you are. Our home is the navy! With our friends, on the ships, in the navy, in these four walls. It doesn't extend beyond that.

"Or do you have the feeling that you belong to Pola, to Dalmatia . . . ? There is a lot that makes you feel at home: the sun, the sea, the smell of the herbs, if you will, the songs of the drunks. But the people? They are as strange to us as we are to them. Down here we have always been the usurper who must be tolerated because there is no other way out, but toward whom you cannot have heartfelt affection. We are not welcome here—and you can feel that."

He cries out, "We would actually have no homeland at all! Can you imagine? We'd have no navy, no sea! Then for us everything is finished; then you can go peddling for a home!"

We have arrived at his cabin. He takes two glasses and a bottle out of the cupboard and pours out the plum brandy.

"Well, cheers . . . maybe I am being too pessimistic!"

"But if you are right? Then let's long for a green forest, for something other than never-ending olive trees and cypresses, for a people who speak German and understand us, for spring water and everything that goes with it . . . and hardly are you there and have it all, then you are drawn back to the sea, so you are at home everywhere and nowhere. That is the fate of the Austrian naval officer. . . . But tomorrow is another day. Shall we shoot pistols again?"

"Yes, splendid! Those loafing *Komitadschis* should see that we can hit the target, too!"[5]

"Good night!"

Forty. **Durazzo**

The Austrians at the Albanian Front have to retreat because Bulgaria refuses to help and the Austrian army, decimated by malaria, can no longer hold the Front. On the 28th of September, they get the order to evacuate within two weeks.

The first evacuation transports leave from Durazzo. The available steamers bring the sick and wounded as well as supplies to the Bocche, and destroyers as well as torpedo boats escort the ships. They barely have two weeks' time; it all must happen as quickly as possible. The vessels are immediately rushed out again, and hardly have time to replenish their coal. The flotilla gives her all to help her land-based comrades.

It is like the last exertion of our strength.

Durazzo lies on the northern end of a five-mile wide bay that is open to the sea. In front of the city three steamers are moored at the dock and are loading. Two old destroyers, *Dinara* and *Sharpshooter* ride at anchor there with torpedo boat *87*, ready to escort the ships to the Bocche.

Suddenly twenty enemy planes approach from the sea. More and more, one after the other, they head for the ships. Enraged, the shore battery and the vessels defend themselves. A sailing ship is hit by bombs and burns. It is loaded with precious aircraft bombs, and the destroyers dispatch firefighting detachments over to save the precious cargo.

Suddenly smoke clouds rise from the horizon. In the north, west, and south, there is a forest of masts. There must be countless ships that the Allies summoned up to take pathetic Durazzo.

Fig. 33. S.M.U. 5 sunk by an encounter with mines

Every means of escape is blocked; our ships cannot leave the bay. Only a hospital ship weighs her anchor and steers out of the harbor, clearly distinguishable by the red stripes on the ship's side and the red cross.

Soon the enemy ships have approached. Three armored cruisers, four light cruisers, fifteen destroyers, fifteen motorboats, and more than thirty planes are approaching, while outside a battleship with destroyer protection gives them security toward the sea. Facing them are the land batteries with their small caliber cannons and their three little K.u.K. vessels.

The light cruisers fire at the city, hangers, and dock simultaneously with the oncoming planes, and immediately afterward the armored cruisers fire their heaviest at the steamers, while the enemy destroyers break through and attack the three vessels. These succeed in outmaneuvering the torpedoes and, together with the land batteries, they fend off the storm.

Fig. 34. Thanks to her design, a German U-boat that ran into a mine could reach home in this condition

The cruisers form two lines, and, crossing back and forth in front of the bay, they concentrate a hail of shells on our vessels.

These vessels travel wildly and independently, back and forth in the large bay, steering in a zigzag pattern to impede the enemy's aim, stopping off and on, then going again at full speed, warding off with their guns the mass attacks from motorboats that keep breaking out between the enemy ships. The attackers practice another method of eluding strikes. Every artilleryman corrects his calculations by observing the splash of his shells striking the water. If these fall too short, he increases the distance; if they fall too wide, he decreases it. The destroyers base their evasion on this principle [called salvo chase[1]]. They steer into the shell splashes and, after the correction of aim, the next salvos fly either over them or they fall short. It requires cool blood to execute this maneuver in the face of a rain of shells and, simultaneously firing, to avoid the torpedoes.

They have already given up hope for their boats, which are riddled with shrapnel. Dead and wounded lie everywhere on deck; it cannot continue this way much longer.

In the middle of the bombardment, there is an immense explosion on the stern of an English cruiser!

What happened?

U-31 had lain in wait overnight south of Durazzo when she saw the enemy armada travel toward Durazzo. American vessels kept her from the route to the enemy; she was discovered through hydrophones and was pelted with depth charges—but Rigele, her commander, persisted and steered toward the group of English cruisers. Then her periscope was discovered and fired at, the whole enemy line turned away, and still Rigele accomplished the feat by sending two torpedoes after the turning *Weymouth* cruiser; the torpedoes demolished her stern and helm. For one moment the battle stopped.

Then a last attack followed from the destroyers, it was again repelled, and Durazzo was free.

One hour after the torpedo encounters of *U-31*, the enemy was out of sight.

Forty-One. To the Last Salute

The wildest news comes tumbling out of Albania. No one can verify it. Guerrilla bands of up to a thousand men, well armed, are forming in the rear of the army. Any scattered groups of soldiers that fall into their hands are plundered, and the officers are murdered without exception. Only those who speak Slavic are let go.

In Durazzo—so the rumor goes—those sick with malaria, with high fevers, must clear out of the hospitals and march off, their blankets on their shoulders, just as they are when they get out of bed. The steamers cannot carry them all. Many are left dying in roadside ditches.

Troops arrive in the Bocche almost nonstop; they storm the railway cars in Zelenika, the terminus of the Bosnian railway. With them come the most horrible and incredible reports, spreading unrest and suspicion everywhere.

One evening some of us U-boat men are invited on board the *Cleopatra*, a steamship of the Austrian Lloyd, the German residence ship. During the entire evening a peculiar wistful mood prevails, very heartfelt and yet very wistful. And on parting we Austrians encounter deeply sad looks.

The next morning we understand the significance of those looks. We learn from the Germans that Austria-Hungary has surrendered!

Now everything happens in rapid succession.

Cleopatra puts out to sea in the evening, a sorrowful departure from old friends who, with the K.u.K. U-boats, have stuck it out to the end.

But there is no time to give in to emotion. Within the individual nationalities, discord springs up: Slavs against Hungarians and Italians, Germans against Czechs. Bolshevist members of all races and nations agitate for general chaos.

And above all this—burning in everyone and irrepressible—is the longing for the homeland.

Reports arrive that, on their way home, the disbanded troops of the Isonzo Front ravaged and plundered through the valleys of Tirol and Kärnten; the men from those areas get restless.

The German U-boats go home. Some, which are not in running order, are blown up and sunk.

No one knows any details. That is what torments us most.

The officers fear that the enemy fleets will force their way into the Bocche, so they don't feel secure with their crews anymore. Insubordination begins on all the ships. For months the men have heard from undercover agitators that it is the officers who have caused the war, that they artificially prolonged it for so long—all the mistrust is directed against them.

Then an order arrives from the Emperor: no armed intervention against insubordination or lack of discipline!

Therefore you can only negotiate with the crew.

Then the 30th of October dawns.

By the order of His Majesty the Emperor and King, the navy is informed in sparse language: the entire navy, the vessels and floating fleet installations, and all construction on land passes into ownership of the new Yugoslavian state. The non-South Slavs are free to continue serving under the new flag. Everyone else is granted permanent leave.

In the Bocche we are to continue normal duty until the final surrender order has been accomplished per instructions.

Rumor has it that the Yugoslavs took over three war loans in exchange. No one knows whether or not the South Slavs will be a state in the framework of the monarchy.

The surrender order is from the Emperor, and so the ships and boats are not sunk.

Now the Yugoslavians lord it over their old comrades, and these men lose any desire to continue serving in the Yugoslavian navy. Ironically, the Yugoslavians badly need their former comrades.

No ship, no torpedo boat, is capable of travel in the next few days. The telephone barely functions in a makeshift fashion.

The effect of the Emperor's order to the crew is the same everywhere: they only want to go home! Only the staff and the regular officers grasp the meaning of the tragedy; they see the misery coming.

A month's wages, a blanket, and tinned goods for fourteen days are granted; that is the farewell after long years of service and war.

The wildest rumors circulate; the majority of them are contradictory.

The Bosnian railway has been supposedly torn up for many kilometers, yet, in contrast, every day soldiers and sailors return from leave in the interior with no idea of the capitulation.

Now everyone wants to go home by train!

It is rumored again: a troop transport of two hundred Germans has been massacred in Bosnia by guerrilla bands. Also the green guerillas from the forests of the Banat have blocked the Save Bridge with guns and are pillaging everything.[1]

This news is not confirmed by any side, and a strong distrust of the Yugoslavs grows; it is rumored that they want to hold back the Austrians in order to hand them over to the Allies as prisoners!

Then news of an armistice comes. But even these reports are contradictory. Nowhere anything definitive, always only: "it is rumored . . ."

"It is rumored" also that the guerrilla bands are on their way into the Bocche, and the new Yugoslavian Fleet command is afraid of a flood of returning guerilla army and of murder and slaughter.

So the Yugoslavians appeal to the Allied fleet in Corfu and invite them to occupy the Bocche to maintain order. The Allies accept and request a destroyer to meet them at the harbor entrance to pilot them through the mines.

But the Yugoslavians cannot fully man a destroyer alone. In addition, the harbor command announces that they would shoot at the enemy ships from the forts. So the Allies must be telegraphed to cancel.

Now it is rumored again that the armistice is still not concluded and the Yugoslavians had only called the enemy fleet because they feared the old navy would seize the ships again.

During this entire time the U-boats are outside the harbor, covering the evacuation of the troops from Albania.

Then we hear the terms of the armistice: the six modern ships of the Austrian fleet, all new destroyers and torpedo boats, are to be presented at Venice for surrender.

Officers as well as men refuse to go.

The Yugoslavians want to save the fleet for themselves and send a destroyer with a deputy of the Zagreb assembly to Corfu to negotiate. They now consider themselves joined to the Allies.

The French now promise free escort. But in spite of a promised high salary, no non-Slav is willing to bring a vessel there.

The harbor command recently gave orders to fire on every departing ship.

An ungodly confusion reigns!

Meanwhile, at the U-boat station, it is business as usual. Although already "on leave" by imperial order, I take up command again to maintain order and am greeted by an enthusiastic "Bravo!" from those reporting for duty.

Those leaving clear a Lloyd steamship, the *Hapsburg*, and go on board. They burn secret orders and install a signal station. Everyone takes along a pistol; provisions and uniforms are distributed. The men are also given their pay. Everything proceeds in perfect order.

Only a few of the Yugoslavian petty officers here have a hostile attitude. In particular, the radio station on the *Hapsburg* arouses ill feeling; after all, it is "Yugoslavian property."

Then just at the right moment the word "guests" appears. A "guest" still has great meaning in the South Slav region, and everyone calms down. An emigrant committee forms. The journey home should proceed orderly. To achieve this, the crew is to send two spokesmen. The U-boat men select me as their station commander and the commander of *U-31*.

One U-boat after another reports back. The majority of them know absolutely nothing of recent events. Everyone awaits the word: war or armistice.

On the night of November 1 the order comes:

The next morning at 8:00 the Austro-Hungarian flag is to be raised for the last time with a twenty-one-gun salute and thereafter lowered forever.

And to this funeral we all turn out to give last honors to our red, white, and red flag. Under her our fathers and forefathers had fought gloriously at Lissa, Helgoland, and on innumerable occasions for more than 140 years and never were defeated. Wherever our flag was hoisted, she fought true to old, passed-down traditions, and was present at so many victories. Now she is to be raised over the stern of a warship for the last time.

Slowly and solemnly I personally raise the flag, wait for the gun salute, and take her down again. For the very last time!

Tears stream down every face. A sobbing is heard all around, as if it were the burial of a most beloved one.

But once more the beloved colors appear. *U-14* enters the Bocche with her flag waving. Tirelessly, the U-boats have held out to the end in their sworn duty.

To the last salute of our flag.

Notes

Introduction

1. Edwyn Gray, *The Devil's Device* (Annapolis, MD: Naval Institute Press, 1991), 180.

2. Agathe's husband John Whitehead was the son of Robert Whitehead, who invented the torpedo.—Trans.

3. Gray, *Devil's Device*, 181.

4. S.M.S.: Seiner Majestät Schiff, or, His Majesty's Ship.—Trans.

5. Because there were so many nationalities under the Austrian flag, some of the men had to learn German to be able to function in the navy. They made up counting songs with simple folk melodies to help them learn the language. These were the songs Georg taught his children.—Trans.

6. The same Seyffertitz is mentioned later in this book; the two men remained good friends for years.—Trans.

7. *The World of the Trapp Family* by William Anderson. Published by Anderson Publications, 1998.

8. The Anschluss was the annexation of Austria to Germany, March 12/13, 1938.—Trans.

1. Between the Islands

1. S.M.: Seiner Majestät Schiff, or His Majesty's Ship.—Trans.

2. Sirocco: wind from the south; bora: wind from the north.—Trans.

2. U-Boats Mobilized

1. Bocche di Cattaro: the Bay of Cattaro, colloquially called "the Bocche."

2. The Lovčen is the highest mountain of Montenegro.

3. The boats are painted black as camouflage.

3. *Léon Gambetta*

1. Because there was not enough room on board the U-boats for the whole crew to sleep simultaneously, the navy provided residence ships for them when they were in port.—Trans.

2. The right of capture: establishment about the seizure of enemy goods, cargo vessels, and their cargo.

3. Conning tower: the low observation tower of a submarine, in which is located the hatch, or entrance.—Trans.

4. A major French fleet unit displacing 12,500 tons with four 19 cm guns and sixteen 16 cm guns.—Trans.

4. Letters

1. This girl attended the Bürgerschüle, a middle school to prepare for a trade.—Trans.

2. Prügelkrapfen: a Viennese pastry specialty.

3. K.u.K.: Kaiserliche und Könige, Emperor and King; i.e., Austro-Hungarian.—Trans.

4. Lissa: a well-known sea battle.—Trans.

6. Trip to the Hinterland

1. She is Irish.—Trans.

2. Himmelblauer Höllteufel: literally, "Sky blue hell devil."—Trans.

7. The Bomb Exploded

1. The Isonzo is the river in Italy that forms the border between it and Austro-Hungary.—Trans.

9. *Giuseppe Garibaldi*

1. Dubrovnik was called Ragusa by the Italians until 1918.—Trans.

10. *Nereide*

1. Sixty degrees Celsius is equivalent to 140 degrees Fahrenheit.—Trans.

2. Oakum is a fiber used to caulk boats, which swells when wet.—Trans.

3. The telephone buoy is one that can be released from the interior of the boat when she lies on the bottom and needs help. It contains a telephone and a bright light to signal.

11. The Prize

1. Vengo: I come.

18. Deck Paint

1. The richly decorated Achilleion Palace on Corfu was the summer retreat of Empress Elisabeth of Austria, owned at this time by Kaiser Wilhelm, Emperor of Germany.—Trans.

2. Because the *Curie* had been sunk and her engine exposed to salt water, the cylinders would need to be rebored when necessary to function properly.—Trans.

19. Bypassing the Official Channels

1. Admiral Haus is the Fleet commander.

21. Reconstruction in the Arsenal

1. Penelope's tapestry refers to Homer's *Odyssey*, in which Penelope unraveled every night what she had woven during the day.—Trans.

22. The First Steamers

1. Cerigo and Cerigotto are islands of southern Greece located south of the Peloponnesus.—Trans.

24. Fog

1. Mount Aetna is an active volcano on the island of Sicily.—Trans.

25. The Two Greeks

1. Gugelhupfs are Austrian cakes.—Trans.

27. One Comes, the Other Goes

1. Bácsi means "uncle" in Hungarian.

28. Gjenović

1. Fallkiel: a keel that can be released to make the boat lighter.—Trans.

2. "Wazachiten" is derived from "wird sich hüten," which is colloquial for people who want to avoid the draft. They see to it that they will not go to war. Information courtesy of Maria F. von Trapp.—Trans.

29. Otranto

1. Hawsers: tow lines.—Trans.

2. God's eye: light-sensitive night binoculars made by Zeiss.

30. Loot

1. Mitzerl: Little Mitzi. Mitzi is a nickname for Maria.—Trans.

2. Schatzerl: Little Sweetheart.—Trans.

3. Naptha: a colorless, volatile petroleum distillate.—Trans.

4. A Wassermann blood test is a test for syphilis.—Trans.

31. Entertainment on Board

1. To "shoot the sun" is to measure the sun's altitude with the sextant.

32. U-Boat Trap

1. "What one cannot identify one must regard as suspicions."—Trans.

2. Arnauld de la Perière was a highly successful World War I German U-boat commander.—Trans.

33. Sheet Lightning

1. Sheet lightning appears as a general illumination over a broad surface, reflecting the lightning of a distant thunderstorm. Here it is used metaphorically, referring to the political situation and the crumbling monarchy.—Trans.

2. A.O.K.: Armee Oberkommando, or German Army Command.—Trans.

36. Internal Duty

1. Schnitzel: veal cutlets.—Trans.

2. Head: toilet.—Trans.

3. Cogo: Italian for "cook."

37. Intermezzo

1. Kaiser Wilhelm II, Emperor of Germany, Prince of Prussia.—Trans.

38. In the East

1. The Russian armistice occurred in December 1917.—Trans.

2. Schmarrn is an Austrian dish of raisin pancakes sprinkled with sugar and served with applesauce. Here it is used as an expression, more like "Baloney!" Information courtesy of Eleonore von Trapp Campbell.—Trans.

3. The Iron Gate is a narrow, canyonlike gorge on the Danube River; one of two such places on the entire river. It marks the beginning of the lower Danube.—Trans.

39. The Fire Goes Out

1. "Gott erhalte Gott beschütze": "God keep you, God protect you," the imperial Austrian national anthem, sung to the melody of the second movement of Haydn's Emperor Quartet. Information courtesy of Eleonore von Trapp Campbell.—Trans.

2. Hilfe!: Help!—Trans.

3. German U-boat commander Arnauld de la Perière.—Trans.

4. The enemy now is also the agents in each nationality who want to break away from the monarchy.—Trans.

5. Komitadschis: guerilla bands.—Trans.

40. Durazzo

1. Editor/translator's note.

41. To the Last Salute

1. The Banat is a fertile, low-lying region extending through Hungary, Romania, and Yugoslavia.—Trans.

9 780803 213500